THE MYSTERY OF THE SEVEN VOWELS

THE MYSTERY
OF THE
SEVEN VOWELS

*In Theory
and
Practice*

by Joscelyn Godwin

PHANES PRESS

98 97 96   5 4 3 2

Published by Phanes Press, PO Box 6114, Grand Rapids, MI 49516, USA.

Find us online at: *http://www.phanes.com*

Library of Congress Cataloging-in-Publication Data

Godwin, Joscelyn.
    The mystery of the seven vowels : in theory and practice / by
Joscelyn Godwin.
        p.   cm.
    Includes bibliographical references.
    ISBN 0-933999-85-2 (alk. paper) — ISBN 0-933999-86-0
(pbk. : alk. paper)
    1. Vowels—Psychic aspects. I. Title.
BF1442.V68G63   1991
133—dc20   90-47432
                                                                CIP

This book is printed on alkaline paper which conforms to the permanent paper standard developed by the National Information Standards Organization.

Printed and bound in the United States

Contents

Mapping the Vowels

Few things in our daily lives are more mysterious than the vowels; few things more essential than these forms through which we shape our speech. As close to us as our own breath, almost as intimate as our thoughts, the vowels are hidden by their very proximity, like the object one searches for while clutching it in one's hand. Yet once they are noticed, paths open up on every side, leading to unsuspected revelations of sound, sense, and symbolism. This small book, which I believe is the first one on the subject in English, is intended to point out some of those paths.

Without the vowels, we would be in a sorry state, having to talk to one another in hums and clicks, hisses and groans, as the beasts do: a possibility, but not an alluring one. A... E... I... O... U... As we listen to the familiar sounds, which the inner ear of our imagination is even now forming as we read them, we may wonder what it is that actually distinguishes one vowel from another. It is not in the air coming from the lungs, which is the prime matter of our speech. Nor is it to be found in the vocal chords that flank the air-passage and vibrate with the current of breath to sound high notes or low. It is in the mouth that tone is transmuted into word, music into meaning. This is the vestibule of the body, open on one side to the world, and on the other to those dark chambers which so few of us understand or are even aware of. The mouth has a dual role, and its two functions mirror each other. First, it is the place where food is worked on by teeth and tongue and converted into fit nourishment for the body. Second, it is the place where the raw sounds of our vocal chords are worked into language, fit nourishment for the world of ideas that surrounds us.

Though the English alphabet names only five or six vowels, dictionaries give phonetic symbols for about twenty, and experts distinguish many dozens. Theoretically their number is limitless, since vowels merge imperceptibly into one another just as musical pitches do. But although pitch is an infinite field, musical convention requires it to be divided into discrete points—in Western music, to twelve different notes per octave—in order to play its particular games with them. The game of language likewise selects only a few vowel-shades as the currency of its conventions: a different currency in each country, or even in each class and district. Then it represents these by an even more limited number of symbols.

Consequently, the written vowels of any language are only a poor approximation of the spoken ones; no symbolic scheme is equal to the subtle differences so obvious in speech. For example, the initial A of the word "actually" becomes a U in Northern English (uctually); a short E in the "Oxford" accent (ectually); a short I to the stage Frenchman (ictually) and an O to the Swede (octually); and in the Southern drawl of the United States, a froglike noise in the back of the throat. When the pioneer of speech studies, Sir Richard Paget, compared the fourteen vowels of his own "Southern English" or "Public School" pronunciation to a set of thirteen vowels pronounced by a French speaker, he found only one (tout or who) that was identical in both lists,[1] though both languages are content to use the same five or six symbols.

Confronted with the elusive and flexible nature of this phenomenon, various researchers have tried to set out the vowels in some logical order, or to map them in more than one dimension. Certain extreme positions of the mouth then serve as the coordinates, or the boundaries. One such limit is the widest possible cavity, with the widest possible aperture: the AH as performed for doctors and dentists. Another is the widest inside cavity coupled with the smallest aperture: a pinhole OO so exaggerated that no one would use it in ordinary speech. The tightly-squeezed EE is a third limit, with the tongue at the roof of the mouth and the lips forming a thin smile.

Having established these three limits, one can explore the wide range of intermediate vowel-colors for which our alphabet furnishes only an approximate notation. Beginning with the AH of c*a*lm, one can either move the tongue forward and the lips into a grin until the point of *ea*t is reached; or else one can constrict the lips while keeping the tongue down, eventually reaching the third coordinate of h*oo*t. To avoid ambiguity, I follow the principle of showing every vowel in the context of a word.

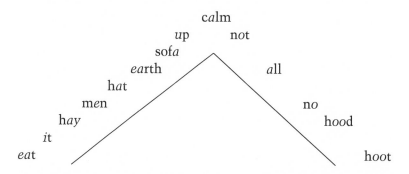

These are a fairly comprehensive set of fourteen English vowels, arranged as they often are in pyramid shape. But in order to complete the base, one has to call on foreign languages, such as French:

s*i* f*i*lle t*u* d*eux* o*eu*f m*o*t m*ou*

or German, where the characteristic sounds of *über* and *möchte* are also present.

This vowel-triangle, adequate as it may be for elementary discussion, takes no account of nasality, the factor that distinguishes sof*a* and not from the French *un* and *on*, and which marks much American diction. The degree to which the nasal cavity is allowed to resonate, by opening the soft palate, might be added as an extra dimension to make the triangle into a tetrahedron. Nor does throat-resonance, so audible in the Scandinavian tongues, appear on it. Finally, the whole concept of a map of sustained vowel-sounds would make nonsense to speakers of a tonal language such as Chinese, where the vowels are always in motion. This much is given as preface, lest the reader take too seriously the artificial limits imposed by five- or seven-voweled alphabets, or by the speech habits of Western cultures. Nevertheless, when we turn from how the vowels are formed to how they are received by the ear, we make an acoustical, even a musical discovery of some significance.

Acoustics

The physicists tell us that what strikes the ear of the listener to speech or song is a series of pressure-changes in the air, arranged in complicated wave-patterns. These patterns record the irregular "noises" of the consonants and the regular "tones" of the intervening vowels. Even in speech, every vowel possesses a definite musical pitch (or a glissando from one pitch to another), as one can prove by gradually slowing down one's speaking until every vowel is prolonged. But it cannot be these fundamental pitches that govern or are governed by the vowels. If it were, a singer could not articulate the whole range of vowels on practically any pitch, singing a scale to c*a*lm, to h*oo*t, to m*e*, etc. The differences must reside somewhere else.

The only possible place for the acoustical definition of the vowels, if the fundamentals are excluded, is the harmonics. One of the first things learnt in acoustics, or in speculative music, is that a tone carries with it a spectrum of more or less audible harmonics, which occupy certain invariant intervals above it. The sequence of intervals is dictated by the whole-number series, either applied as multipliers to the fundamental vibration-count, or as fractions to the fundamental string-length. For example, the first sixteen harmonics of low bass C, produced by a four-foot string vibrating 64 times a second, are as follows:

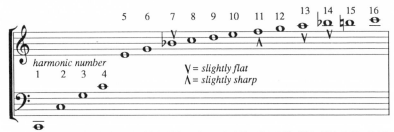

64 128 192 256 320 384 448 512 576 640 704 768 832 896 960 1024
cycles per second

Example 1: The first 16 tones of the Harmonic Series on C

It is the harmonics that characterize the tone qualities of
instruments, and account for the fact that this low C would sound
perceptibly different on a cello, a bass clarinet, a French horn, or an
organ diapason. The peculiar tone-quality of the clarinet, for
example, is due to the fact that it sounds only the odd-numbered
harmonics. The flute's pure tone comes from having nearly all of its
energy in the fundamental. The soft notes of the French horn have
a weak fundamental and a strong second harmonic. One hears the
tone-quality of an instrument without being consciously aware of
its acoustical cause. Likewise, in hearing vowels, one's ear is
actually registering harmonics, of whose existence most people are
altogether unconscious.

It used to be thought that the parallel between instrumental
timbre and vowels could be taken further, namely that similar to
an instrument, each vowel had a characteristic arrangement of
harmonics, no matter what pitch it was sung on. Thus perhaps h*oo*t
is always fluty, h*ea*t always stringlike in tone. The debate lasted
until the early part of this century, when the acoustician Dayton
Clarence Miller settled the matter in favor of the alternative
theory. Miller confirmed, with the help of vowel-photography,
what Sir Charles Wheatstone had proposed in 1837 and Hermann
Helmholtz had also deduced on the basis of his experiments with
resonators: that a vowel does not have a constant harmonic spectrum, but rather certain "formants" or resonant pitch-areas that
favor any harmonic that happens to fall within them.[2] Paget had

already discovered this for himself in the 1880s, as an undergraduate at Magdalen College, Oxford. The college chaplain's voice, he writes, "was melodious and resonant, and when he intoned the services in Chapel the harmonics of the note on which he was intoning varied with each change of vowel and performed bugle-calls of an almost militant character."[3]

Vowels depend on resonance. If one sings up the scale into a large bottle or jar, or in a tiled bathroom, there will come a particular note at which the vessel resonates and amplifies the sound. The Roman architectural writer Vitruvius tells (*De Architectura* V) that in the ancient theaters, bronze jars tuned to a wide range of pitches were placed around the stage and auditorium in order to amplify the voices by just such sympathetic resonance. In an analogous way, the cavities in the head and throat form a series of resonators. Those of the throat and nose can be opened or shut at will, while the mouth is subject to the finest adjustment, often being divided by the tongue into two regions with different resonances. Any given position of the cavities will favor a particular set of pitches. With his usual gift for memorable imagery, Paget wrote that "Considered as a musical instrument, the human voice is really a little orchestra of wind instruments—a reed (of the oboe type) and two, three, or four muted whistles (of the ocarina type). In whispered speech the reed does not play; in voiced speech the reed plays *through* the ocarinas. In the case of nasal vowels all four ocarinas are used—in other cases two only are essential."[4]

Since these cavities are rather small, their resonances are on the whole high-pitched, even higher than the range of a soprano voice. So, unlike the experiment in which one sings into a large jar, it is not the fundamental tones of the vocal chords that are enhanced, but certain of their harmonics. Whatever harmonics are closest to a given resonance-area will be strengthened to the extent of sounding several times louder than the fundamental itself. For instance, Dayton Miller found that the chief resonances of the vowels m*a*, m*aw*, m*ow*, and m*oo* amplify a single harmonic so that it contains as much as 90 percent of the total energy of the sound.[5]

So far, there is general agreement that it is the resonant areas that give the vowels their individuality. But consensus breaks down as soon as the attempt is made to quantify the formants of each vowel. Miller found only one for the vowels mentioned above; Paget found two different regions for all the vowels; the *Encyclopedia Britannica* currently gives three. There is further disagreement on the exact placement of the resonance areas. Early reports[6] diverged partly because of the different languages analyzed (English, German, and Dutch), and partly because of the various methods used: hollow resonators, tuning forks, or simply listening intently to one's own or another's voice. Some were based on whispering alone. Even after 1950, with the application of phonographic methods and spectograms, there was still only a broad statistical correlation between results as published in scientific reference works. Only now is it becoming possible, with the aid of computers, to analyze the acoustics of cavities as complex as those of the speaking apparatus, and to define their resonances. Quantitative analysis of the vowels will always founder on the fact that every voice is unique. One need only consider how readily one can recognize familiar voices from a single word, a cough, or even from the intake of breath, to realize how individual is every person's resonance system or "voice print," and how finely tuned one's ear must be in order to distinguish between them.

One can experience the connection of vowels with harmonics through a simple experiment. The best vowels for this purpose are those with low resonances, who and no. Beginning at the bottom of one's voice range, sing slowly up a scale, listening for the emergence of the upper harmonics. If the partials are not readily audible, try singing a note, then without changing the position of the mouth, send the air through it without the vocal chords, as if whistling. Listen carefully to the pitch of the whistle-tone: it is approximately that of the harmonic to be listened for. Slight adjustments of the tongue and lips enable one to focus the resonance so as to amplify the favored partial. Here are the results of my own experiment, first conducted not in the helpful acoustics of a chapel, but in the course of a long solitary car journey. The notes in the bass clef are the fundamental tones, those in the treble clef the most prominent and audible harmonics. One can see that each vowel has a resonant range of about a major third.

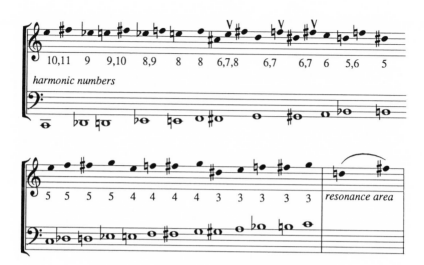

Example 2.i: Primary resonance of the vowel OOH

Example 2.ii: Primary resonance of the vowel OH

Some people have gone so far as to execute two-part inventions with fundamentals and harmonics—a vocal polyphony exploited to marvelous effect in recent years by David Hykes and his Harmonic Choir. But this is more practicable for male than for female voices. For the higher one sings, the choice of harmonics to occur in the resonant area becomes more and more limited, until it is only the fundamental itself that can be amplified by the primary vowel-resonance. This probably accounts for the "hooty" quality of some voices, especially those of boy sopranos, in the notes toward the top of the treble staff; also for the fact that a coloratura soprano's words are virtually incomprehensible. Women and boys typically speak well below the range in which Western composers require them to sing, thereby availing themselves of a richer spectrum of harmonics.

The findings of acoustics compel one to admit the surprising fact that every time one hears language, whether sung or spoken, one is unconsciously perceiving an intricate melody of high harmonics, and that this is the very thing that carries meaning and enables us to understand one another. Whether we are aware of it or not, this proves that all humans are innately and actively musical, constantly picking out the softest and most transient of tones and discriminating between their nicest shades. This makes nonsense, incidentally, of the concept of "tone-deafness," in the commonly accepted sense of being unable to distinguish one pitch from another. If anyone really lacked this capacity, they could never understand a word anyone said. The so-called tone-deaf are usually people who have been less quick at matching pitches than the majority of children, and have been silenced by school-teachers.

Another conclusion to be drawn from the unconscious hearing of vowel-resonances is that we must have an inborn familiarity with the harmonic series. Somewhere in our perceptive mechanism, the harmonics of vocal tones are being analyzed and presented to our consciousness as vowels. The intervals of the harmonic series must be deeply imbued in our unconscious. This is surely the explanation of why people all round the world respond intuitively to the basic harmonic intervals, and why they are at the basis of every musical system. Some people, on first learning about the harmonic series and in hearing it played, feel an instant kinship with this hierarchy of pure intervals. It is, after all, our most direct perception of the numbers which underlie not just the acoustical world, but the whole physical universe.

THREE

Vowels and Planets

Another dimension of the vowels opens up when we learn that in Graeco-Roman antiquity they were made to correspond to the seven Chaldaean planets, i.e. the seven heavenly "wanderers" visible to the naked eye. The first savant to assemble the evidence for this was the Abbé Jean Jacques Barthélemy (1716–95), best known for his immense didactic romance of classical Greece, *Les voyages du jeune Anacharsis en Grèce* (published 1787). Barthélemy was led to explore the sources of classical vowel-lore by his numismatic studies,[7] which had brought to his notice some medals of Gnostic provenance enigmatically inscribed with the seven vowels of the Greek alphabet:

A, α	alpha (a)
E, ε	epsilon (short e)
H, η	eta (long ê)
I, ι	iota (i)
O, o	omicron (short o)
Υ, υ	upsilon (u)
Ω, ω	omega (long ô)

Barthélemy found a parallel to these medals in an inscription in the theater of Miletus (Asia Minor), discovered by English explorers in the seventeenth century. This inscription, though damaged, had evidently had seven columns, each headed by a sequence of seven vowels, followed by a prayer that the city of Miletus and all its inhabitants should be preserved. The first column began ι ε o υ α η ω, then continued with the alphabetical order α ε η ι ο υ ω; the second column had in the corresponding place ε η ι ο υ ω α, and so on in alphabetical order, starting with each vowel in turn, and continuing ". . . holy one, preserve the city of Miletus and all its inhabitants."

These vowel-sequences evidently represented the names of seven powers invoked to preserve the city, and Barthélemy did not doubt that they were the gods of the seven planets. As he says, the fact that there is the same number of vowels and planets would have sufficed to establish an affinity between them in ancient times. He suggests that the inscription might be explained as beginning with a sort of prelude, then invoking each planetary god in turn, so that the meaning of the first would be: "O holy Moon, who art at the head of the other planets Mercury, Venus, Sun, Mars, Jupiter, and Saturn, preserve. . .," etc. A later authority, Franz Dornseiff, says that the lettering of the inscription dates it to the Byzantine era, and that the prayers are consequently addressed to the archangels of Christianity.[8] But where the planets leave off and their tutelary angels begin, who can say? Dornseiff himself mentions that the Archangel Michael is identified with the planet Mercury, and other angel-planet correspondences would become a commonplace of Christian ceremonial magic.

Barthélemy collected several further instances in late classical works of the use of the vowels to denote the planetary gods. One witness was a certain Porphyry (a different person from the famous Neoplatonist[9]) who wrote a commentary on Dionysius of Thrace. He says there that alpha is consecrated to Venus, iota to the Sun, omicron to Mars, upsilon to Jupiter, and omega to Saturn. This leaves two vowels unassigned, epsilon and eta, and two planets, the Moon and Mercury.

For corroboration of these correspondences, Barthélemy next refers to Marcus, a Gnostic philosopher whose doctrines are preserved, along with much other pagan wisdom, by his opponent Saint Irenaeus (circa 130-circa 200 C.E.), in the latter's book against heresies.[10] Marcus explains that the first heaven sounds alpha, the second epsilon, the third eta, the fourth iota, the fifth omicron, the sixth upsilon, the seventh omega.

To summarize: Porphyry and Marcus agree in aligning the four upper heavens with the four latter vowels:

7th heaven	Saturn	omega
6th heaven	Jupiter	upsilon
5th heaven	Mars	omicron
4th heaven	Sun	iota

A possible conclusion is that the three lower heavens correspond to the three initial vowels, and that Porphyry made a mistake about the vowel assigned to Venus. Taking the Egyptian ordering of the planets, which was also that of the Pythagoreans, we might complete the septenary as follows:

3rd heaven	Venus	eta
2nd heaven	Mercury	epsilon
1st heaven	Moon	alpha

Another piece of pagan lore preserved in the Patrologia refers to a similar form of devotion to that of the Miletus tablet. Eusebius of Caesarea (circa 260-340 C.E.) quotes the *Philosophy from Oracles* of Porphyry the Neoplatonist (232/3-circa 305 C.E.), in which is preserved the following oracle of Apollo:

Invoke Hermes and the Sun in the same way,
On the Sun's day, and [invoke] the Moon when her day comes,
Then Cronos and Rhea, and next Aphrodite,
With silent prayer, invented by the greatest mage,
King of the seven notes, known to all.[11]

Later Eusebius adds that it was with the seven vowels that the Jews sought to express the name of God which cannot be spoken, but that they reduced these to four for the use of the multitude.[12] He draws a parallel with a saying he remembers from one of the Wise Men of Greece (who may well be Porphyry again): "The seven vowels celebrate me, the great imperishable God, indefatigable

Father of all. I am the imperishable lyre, having tuned the lyric songs of the celestial vortex."[13] This is a formulation of the beautiful doctrine of astral paganism, according to which the Sun is the leader of the choir of planets, and Apollo's lyre a symbol of the harmony of the spheres.

It is Franz Dornseiff, however, who again cautions against a too cut-and-dried interpretation of ancient correspondences. He cites an invocation in one of the magical papyri of "α ε η ι ο υ ω that rise in the night," heavenly bodies which evidently do not include the sun; they must be the seven stars of the Great Bear, he says, which, in a tradition that goes back to Babylonian times, are confused with the seven planets and even called by their names.[14] This ambiguity—which is the same as that between the Hyperborean and the Delian Apollo—was recognized by the Sabaeans of Harran, that mysterious Hermetic sect which survived into Muslim times. They had seven temples dedicated to the planets, and seem to have originated the correspondences of planets to metals,[15] but their worship also included a liturgy addressed to the Pole Star, around which the Great Bear turns.

We now call a last witness to the divine vowel-names, who is also the oldest and the best-known. This passage comes from the *De Elocutione* of Demetrius (late Hellenistic or early Roman period), who says simply:

> In Egypt the priests, when singing hymns in praise of the gods, employ the seven vowels, which they utter in due succession; and the sound of these letters is so euphonious that men listen to it in place of aulos and cithara.[16]

This shows that by Hellenistic times, Egypt was being credited with this practice of invoking the planetary gods through sounding the vowels. However, the Egyptian language was still being written in hieroglyphs and their derivations, not in alphabetical script. It had no vowels until the fourth century of the Common Era, when the Greek alphabet was adapted to it in the form of Coptic. Somewhat akin to Chinese, the writing of ancient Egypt, and, presumably, its linguistic thought, was based on phonemes (vowel-consonant combinations, for the most part), and not on the analysis of speech into two basic components, vowels and consonants.[17] One might be inclined to dismiss the Egyptian pedigree as a typical symptom of Hellenistic reverence for Egypt as the source of everything holy. This was, after all, the period when the writings of "Hermes Trismegistus" were compiled in Greek and attributed to the most ancient sages of the Black Land. Yet the more the Hermetic writings are studied, the more "Egyptian" they are admitted to be.[18] And we have a comparatively early witness to the Egyptian interest in the structure of language in Plato, writing in the early fourth century B.C.E. In the *Philebus* 18b, Socrates tells of "some god, or divine man, called Theuth in the Egyptian reports," who was the first to analyze the sounds of human speech into three divisions: mutes, semi-vowels, and vowels. The hieratic vowel-lore need not have depended originally on any written form or alphabetical arrangement. Stephen Ronan[19] has suggested that the origin of vowel incantations may lie in attempts to record the utterances of glossolalia (speaking in tongues), a phenomenon well attested in Biblical as well as in modern times. Just as the Pythoness of Delphi would deliver the oracles of Apollo out of her intoxicated trance as a series of incomprehensible sounds (turned by the priests into neat hexameters), so it may be that ecstatic worshippers have been thus moved wherever the spirit may have seized them.

Nicomachus of Gerasa, a Pythagorean of the late first to early second centuries, C.E., seems to be describing a similar practice at the end of this important extract from his *Manual of Harmony*:

> And the tones of the seven spheres, each of which by nature produces a particular sound, are the sources of the nomenclature of the vowels. These are described as unpronounceable in themselves and in all their combinations by wise men since the tone in this context performs a role analogous to that of the monad in number, the point in geometry, and the letter in grammar. However, when they are combined with the materiality of the consonants just as soul is combined with body and harmony

with strings—the one producing a creature, the other notes and
melodies—they have potencies which are efficacious and perfec-
tive of divine things. Thus whenever the theurgists are conducting
such acts of worship they make invocation symbolically with
hissing, clucking, and inarticulate and discordant sounds.[20]

The vowels, according to Nicomachus, symbolize what he
elsewhere calls "the primary sounds emitted by the seven heavenly
bodies."[21] But since the planets exist in ether, not in air, their
sounds are inaudible; hence the vowels are unpronounceable until
they are framed in the material consonants. Seen from another side,
they are the closest our speech can come to the supersensible
world, for they represent the life which comes thence and animates
the inert body of language. As a Pythagorean, Nicomachus has an
intuitive feel for the very place where number—mainspring of the
Pythagorean cosmos—is most essential to language, as explained
in the preceding chapter. Also the sound of whistling, in the
Gnostic and Chaldaean oracular literature, is associated with the
descent of the soul from the higher spheres into the body; hence it
is fitting that theurgists should use it to summon the powers from
those spheres. Probably the grammarian Servius had such rites in
mind when, commenting on the phrase of Virgil "Voce vocans
Hecaten" (*Aeneid* VI, 249), he interpreted it as: "Invoking Hecate
not by words but by *mystic sounds.*"

Digging deeper into the psychogonic and cosmogonic mystery,
we turn again to the Gnostic Marcus:

> When first the Father, the not even the One, beyond all possibility
> of thought and being, who is neither male nor female, willed that
> His ineffability should come into being, and His invisibility take
> form, He opened His mouth and uttered a Word, like unto
> Himself; who, appearing before Him, became the means of His
> seeing what He himself was—namely Himself appearing in the
> form of His own invisibility.[22]

For Marcus, this Word (*logos*) was given in four utterances of 4
+ 4 + 10 + 12 letters, making thirty in all. Later[23] Irenaeus sum-

marizes Marcus's analysis of the twenty-four letters of the Greek alphabet: the nine consonants symbolize the ineffable or soundless elements before manifestation; the eight liquids, the intermediary elements that facilitate creation; the seven vowels, the manifestation of our cosmos with its seven planetary spheres (compare the passage from Plato's *Philebus*, cited above).

Marcus adds that the seven vowels, uniting in harmony, send forth a sound and glorify the world-builder; also, that the echoes of this hymn of glory rise to the Divine Logos, and descend to earth to model and generate the souls of men.[24] Such teaching accords, as one might expect, with the principle of Hermetic astrology: that the soul as it descends into earthly incarnation is imbued by the various planetary energies. These in turn are seven archetypal divisions of the cosmogonic power, known in both Gnostic and Johannine theology as a creative Word or Logos.

Gnosticism recognized that Seven is God's favorite number, recurring on all levels of being. Writing on "Theosophical Symbology," and alluding to one of the engraved gems of the "Abraxas" type, G. R. S. Mead says: "The Gnostic Dragon has seven 'vowels' above its crest. These vowels typify the seven planes of Cosmos, the seven principles in man, and all the septenates in nature." The euphonious sounding of seven vowels is thus a way of reflecting the wholeness of this creative vibration that has formed the cosmos and the planets, as it has informed our own souls.

FOUR

Vowels and Tones

Theuth or Thoth, in Egyptian mythology, was the inventor of writing and of other useful arts and sciences, including magic. In the Hellenistic period he became associated with the name and doctrines of Hermes Trismegistus. One of the most important of the Hermetic doctrines, along with cosmogony and the descent and ascent of the soul, is that of universal correspondence. Finding its most fundamental expression in the reflection of the macrocosm (universe) in the human microcosm, this doctrine was elaborated into a cosmology of multiple planes or fields, related to each other not causally but by reflecting a common pattern or archetype. It is this reflection that makes magic theoretically possible, an action on one plane being able, under certain circumstances, to move by a sort of resonance the entity that corresponds to it on another plane. The sounding of a certain vowel, for instance, might set up a vibration to which a certain planetary energy responds.

In the end, all Hermetic correspondences can be reduced to number. The number seven has its most prominent manifestation in the seven Chaldaean planets; so, everywhere else that sevenness operates, we may expect to find that the members correspond in their own way to the planetary archetypes. In the present instance, we have seen sevenness manifesting in the field of speech as the Greek vowels, and some attempts made to specify which vowel goes with which planet. Given the well-known correspondence of planets to the notes of the musical scale, it is a short step to align the vowels with the seven diatonic tones. Indeed, it would seem especially appropriate to bring these two septenaries together, since both are in the realm of sound.

The first modern scholar to collect the evidence for the vowel-tone connection in antiquity was Thomas Gale, in *Rhetores graeci* (Oxford, 1716, p. 265). Writing on the passage we have cited from Demetrius, Gale referred to the *Hieroglyphics* of Horapollo (II, 29), which states that for the Egyptians, seven letters distributed on two fingers "signify music," and remarked that these seven letters must be the same as the vowels to which Demetrius refers.[25] Gale also cited Cornutus's *De Musis*, Nicomachus, Servius, Porphyry's commentary on Dionysius Thrax, and Saint Irenaeus.

The Abbé Barthélemy, in the article cited in our preceding chapter, suggested that the vowels assigned to the planets must go also with the "celestial lyre." But this observation is far from settling the matter of which vowels to assign to which notes of the scale—for even in antiquity there were several different versions of planet-tone correspondence, and disagreements on so basic a question as whether the highest note of the scale should be assigned to the highest sphere, that of Saturn, or to the fastest planet, namely the Moon. Besides, which of the dozens of possible scales should be chosen? Barthélemy followed Nicomachus, who used two conjunct tetrachords of the Dorian diatonic scale, A G F E D C B, running from Saturn at A down to the Moon at B. He was then able to read the vowels in the Miletus inscription as the notation of a simple melody, qualifying it as *"peu flattant aux oreilles,"*[26] which it surely was to the *galant* taste of 1775.

Barthélemy's interpretation of the vowel-sequences as merely formal invocations of the planetary gods was greatly expanded by the German philologist Ulrich Kopp when he touched on the subject in his *Palaeographia critica*.[27] Kopp agreed that the vowels represent the planetary gods, and that their recitation was intended to make their influences benefic. Inspired by the discovery of an amulet inscribed with ninety Greek vowels in apparently random order, Kopp suggested that these letters were musical notes corresponding to those of Orpheus's seven-stringed lyre; but his reading of their order was in the reverse direction to Barthélemy's, i.e. with the highest tone assigned to the Moon.

Thus we are offered two alternative schemes of vowel-tone

correspondence, of which Barthélemy proposed the first, while Kopp favored the second:

1. *Saturn high*			2. *Moon high*		
Saturn	omega	A	Moon	alpha	A
Jupiter	upsilon	G	Mercury	epsilon	G
Mars	omicron	F	Venus	eta	F
Sun	iota	E	Sun	iota	E
Venus	eta	D	Mars	omicron	D
Mercury	epsilon	C	Jupiter	upsilon	C
Moon	alpha	B	Saturn	omega	B

A third scheme had meanwhile been conjectured by the great esotericist Fabre d'Olivet (1767–1825), author of *La Langue Hébraïque restituée*, but was not published until 1844. Fabre d'Olivet's description, set in the context of antique history, reads as follows:

> At the moment when the Shepherds dismembered the Indian Empire and formed the famous sect that gave birth to the Phoenician nation, it seems that they chose to designate the seven diatonic tones of their musical system by the seven vowels of their alphabet, in such a way that the first of these vowels, *alpha* or A, was applied to the Cyprian principle F, which they regarded as first, and the last, *ain*, which the Greeks rendered by *omega* and we by *ou*, was applied to the Saturnian principle B, which they considered as the last. One may believe that it was as a natural consequence of this way of notating the two musical strings, assimilated to the two principles of the Universe, that was born the famous dictum put in the mouth of the Supreme Being to designate his omnipotence and immensity: "I AM THE ALPHA AND THE OMEGA."
>
> However, either because the Phoenicians had two methods of notating the tones, or whether they considered them as proceeding by harmonic intervals, B, E, A, D, G, C, F, or by diatonic ones, B, C, D, E, F, G, A; or because time or political and religious

revolutions caused certain changes in their notation, it is clear
from several passages in ancient writers that the A string, assimilated to the Moon and the tonic of the *common* or Locrian mode,
was notated by the vowel A; so that the entire scale sung from
high to low was solfèged to the seven Phoenician vowels, unknown
today; and in going from high to low it went consequently from
right to left, instead of from low to high and from left to right. The
Shepherds, in breaking away from the Indian Empire, adopted this
method which they passed on to those who depended directly or
indirectly on them. The Egyptians, the Arabs, the Assyrians, the
Greeks, the Etruscans received it and conserved it for a longer or
shorter time according to circumstances. The Arabs and all those
who accepted the yoke of Islam follow it to this day.[28]

It should be mentioned that these "Phoenicians" are not those
of profane history, but of Fabre d'Olivet's esoteric and "philosophical" history of prehistoric times.[29] Their original scheme, as
he describes it, would have given correspondences based on the
progression of fifths, but the only vowels that can be inserted with
certainty are the first and the last:

3. *"Phoenician" scheme, by fifths*

omega [Saturn]	B
	E
[lost Phoeni-	A
cian vowels]	D
	G
	C
alpha [Moon]	F

Thereafter, as Fabre d'Olivet gives us to understand, this
scheme was replaced by the one we have numbered 2, previous
page.

In one of those synchronisms of which intellectual history
seems to be full, there was another attempt during Fabre d'Olivet's
period to find a system of correspondence based not on their given

order in the Greek alphabet, but on the experiential and physical aspect of the vowels. This was made in 1811 by one of the most astonishing of the German Romantic philosophers, Johann Jacob Wagner (1771–1841).[30] Attempting to incorporate the vowels in his grand scheme of correspondences based on a universal "Law of Four," Wagner places A at the bottom, as the most "subjective" and open vowel whose sound comes from deep down; at the top he puts O, which issues from the most external part of the mouth and is thus the most "objective" vowel. Mediating between this Alpha-Omega pair are E and U (the latter described as merely a muted O). Wagner's fixed idea about the number four prevents him from including any further vowels in his scheme, but at least he has given the extremes alpha and omega some sort of empirical basis. They are of course the limits of one of the sides of our vowel-triangle, as given in Chapter 2.

J. J. Wagner agrees with Fabre d'Olivet's Phoenicians in setting alpha as the lower limit of the vowel-scale, omega as the upper limit, with the other vowels in between. But the Greek alphabet did not have seven vowels until classical times: upsilon and omega were formally adopted only in 403 B.C.E. Greek originally had five vowels, like the Minoan Linear B script and the Phoenician alphabet (following modern authorities rather than Fabre d'Olivet). It seems, therefore, that every effort to align the vowels according to the Greek order is artificial. Such a correspondence does not necessarily demand a written alphabet, merely the recognition of seven different vowel-sounds; as was pointed out in Chapter 3, there is no reason that the connection might not have been made in a non-alphabetical culture, such as the Egypt which is reputedly the source of this, as of all Hermetic doctrine. It is possible that the Greek alphabet only adapted itself in classical times—and perhaps deliberately—to the expression of this time-honored septenary, and that by then the authentic pronunciations had been lost.

Repeated experimentation, both alone and in groups, has convinced me that the place to seek for practical, rather than theoretical, correspondences is not in the alphabetical order of vowels, whether Hebrew, Greek, Latin, or English, but in their natural, acoustic pitch. The latter places EE at the top, AH in the middle, and OH or OO at the bottom, no matter what pitch boundaries are set.[31]

Jean Thamar, who was a contributor to the periodical *Etudes Traditionnelles* during its domination by René Guénon, makes a connection between this acoustic "scale of vowels" from the low U to the high I (pronounced EE in French), and the sevenfold scale. He writes:

> The first method of forming the scale, which is also called "proportional" because it assumes the division of a sounding length (string or pipe), takes as its point of departure the psychological interpretation of the intervals: that is the Hindu and Arab method. The second, which one may call "cyclic" on account of the indefinite spiral formed by the superimposed fifths, has a purely acoustic point of departure; it is the Chinese method. . .
>
> Greece practised both methods: the second produces the so-called "harmonic" or "Pythagorean" scale and also controls the succession of the days of the week, thus:

> Monday (Moon—C or Do)
>
>   Tuesday (Mars—G or Sol)
>
> Wednesday (Mercury—D or Re)
>
>   Thursday (Jupiter—A or La)
>
> Friday (Venus—E or Mi)
>
>   Saturday (Saturn—B or Si)
>
> Sunday (Sun—F or Fa)

> Thus the week was conceived (doubtless by Hermeticism) as the terrestrial trace of the "harmony of the spheres." Note here that the scale of vowels, going from the lowest one, U, to the highest one, I, passing notably through the most central one, A, produces a succession that partially coincides with that of the vowels contained in the syllables of the Latin and French scale: Ut (=Do), Re, Mi, Fa, Sol, La, Si. Perhaps the coincidence was originally exact.[32]

It is curious that Thamar does not mention the well-known source of the solfège syllables: an eighth-century plainsong hymn to John the Baptist, of which each line begins on the appropriate note:

Ut queant laxis
*Re*sonare fibris
*Mi*ra gestorum
*Fa*muli tuorum
*Sol*ve polluti
*La*bii reatum
*S*ancte *I*ohannes

But his is not the first improbable theory of the meaning of these Latin note-names.[33] The difficulty in arriving at any definitive version of such correspondences, or at any reasonable explanation of their origin, is only increased when we turn to the parallel domain of color.

FIVE

Vowels and Colors

It is true that the non-linear nature of the vowels makes them more comparable to color than to tone. In color, as in the vowels, there are certain extreme fixed points, like black and white or three primary colors, while between them runs an infinitely divisible range of shades. Even the fixed points, as in vowel analysis, are subjects of debate; for example between the Newtonians, whose primary postulate is the seven-colored spectrum, and the followers of Goethe's *Farbenlehre,* for whom all colors are modifications of the extremes of black and white.

The most famous attempt at a vowel-color parallel is the one proposed by the poet Arthur Rimbaud, who in his early sonnet (circa 1870) on the vowels (*"A noir, E blanc, I rouge, U vert, O bleu"*) assigns black to A, white to E, red to I, green to U, and blue to O. Much ink has been spilt in trying to explain why Rimbaud chose the colors he did. Perhaps he felt that the openness of the A gives on to the dark cavern of the mouth; it is the first of sounds, the unformed place from which the voice emerges. The French E, verging towards the A of sof*a* when it is not simply mute, is the most indifferent and colorless of the vowels. The intensity of the I (m*ee*t) is like the sharp sting of scarlet, though later in the poem Rimbaud makes it the "purple" of spat-out blood and of penitence. The French U or German ü, so foreign to English mouths, has the greatest range of audible harmonics, mysterious like the inexhaustible greens of nature. Robert Greer Cohn[34] points out its innate tension, combining a bright, acute, male I with a relaxed, open, female receptacle, which is acoustically if not anatomically correct (one pronounces it by holding the mouth in the shape of h*oo*t, then trying to say me). And the deep and resonant O is like the azure bowl of the sky, the limit of our vision as the omega is the end of the Greek alphabet, and, apocalyptically, of all things.

So one might argue. Rimbaud's correspondences may not convince, but there is an intuitive truth to his analogy. One could develop it by imagining the vowels as coloring in the spaces delineated by the consonants, as one might tint a line-drawing; an analogy which, needless to say, is not original. But then black and white would refer to the consonants, and each vowel would have a "true" color. This is in fact the usual assumption of those who have proposed vowel-color correspondences. Hargrave Jennings, in his catch-all book of esoteric lore *The Rosicrucians, their Rites and Mysteries* (1870), offers the following list of vowels aligned with the colors of Newton's spectrum and of heraldry, gems, and planets. (The queries are his own.)

Y.	1. Violet (Red and Blue)—*Most Refrangible Ray.*
	Sanguine. Sardonyx. Dragon's Tail.[35]
W.	2. Indigo (Opaque Blue).
	Purpure. Amethyst (?). Mercury (?).
U.	3. Blue (Azure).
	Sapphire. Jupiter.
O.	4. Green (Yellow and Blue).
	Vert. Emerald. Venus.
I.	5. Yellow.
	Or. Topaz. Gold. Sol.
E.	6. Orange (Red and Yellow).
	Tawny. Tenne. Jacinth. Dragon's Head.
A.	7. Red—*Least Refrangible Ray.*
	Gules. Ruby. Mars.

"Also," he adds unhelpfully, "the Chromatic Scale of seven Musical Notes."[36] There is no telling where Jennings got this system from. What is odd is that the idea of the seven vowels and their correspondences is conspicuously absent from the Western magical tradition. It did not figure in the *Three Books on Natural Magic* of Cornelius Agrippa, nor in the so-called "Magical Calendar of Tycho Brahe," which are the ancestors of most correspondence tables from 1600 to the present. The vowels are not mentioned in Francis Barrett's *The Magus* (1801), itself a compendium that was ransacked by nineteenth century writers, nor do they play any special part in the Kabbalistic system of Eliphas Lévi, the "Archéomètre" of Saint-Yves d'Alveydre, or the symbolism and ceremonies of the "Hermetic Order of the Golden Dawn in the Outer"—a surprising fact, given the Egyptian atmosphere of the latter. Even Aleister Crowley's *Liber 777*, a collection of correspondence tables of unmatched thoroughness, omits them. Interest in the esoteric aspect of the vowels seems to have been limited to a small coterie of French researchers during the nineteenth and twentieth centuries.

How, in any case, are such correspondences ever arrived at, discounting their artificial invention such as I suspect to have been the case with Hargrave Jennings? We can gain some insight into the procedure from a 1897 work by the occultist Paul Sédir (real name Yvon Leloup), who reports some very curious experiments with a medium whom he "plunged into a magnetic sleep," i.e., hypnotized.[37] Somewhat in the spirit of what Rudolf Steiner would later call "spiritual science," Sédir regarded this as a genuine scientific investigation, involving three elements: (1) a sound-producer, (2) a receptive medium, and (3) a recording machine. Only the second element was the "astral light," and the third, the human body. The information obtained took the form of graphic and geometric figures, seen by the hypnotized subject as "inscribed by the sounds on the astral canvas."

The sounds chosen by Sédir for transcription were of two sorts: Hindu mantras, and notes of the piano. His drawings of them are in black and white, but they carry indications of color, and sometimes also of temperature and movement. For example, the Buddhist mantram "OM! MANI PADME HUM!" looked like four interlaced circles in pale green, with a cold sensation to them. The "mantram of the element of ether" was a B-minor arpeggio that took the form of a green ring, its circumferences decorated by blue arrows. The lowest C of the piano was a bright red helmet shape, the C# a blue rectangle with a green point in the center. Then there are the "forms of the Latin alphabet in the solar astral region," made from disks and squares—which unfortunately do not treat the vowels in any systematic way. Incidentally, Sédir's depictions predate by several years the *Thought Forms* of Annie Besant and C. W. Leadbeater (1905), which had the extra appeal of expensive color printing, and seems to have had an influence on the beginnings of abstract art. [38]

Such experiments shed a new light on our subject. Psychically sensitive people can enter a state in which the Hermetic correspondences appear palpable, and if suitably prompted can read them like a book, translating from one medium to another—in this case, from sound into color and form. If requested, Sédir's medium could doubtless have obliged with the correspondences of vowels with tones, with planets—or, for that matter, with the Kings of France or with makes of automobiles. But would they have agreed with those of another medium, especially one thousands of years earlier and in another cultural world? To judge by the variety of proposals we have met already, the answer would be no.

The composer and Theosophist Cyril Scott (1879–1970), writing in 1917, is quite precise about the results of such research, and the different levels on which it may be conducted:

> I would have it noted that the vowels have also their corresponding colours perceptible to the psychic. These are as follows:

Colours:	violet	yellow	indigo	orange
Vowels:	a	e	ee	i
	red	blue	green	
	o	u	oo	

And yet, here again we find that the trained psychic differs from those who associate, by an elementary form of clairvoyance much tainted by imagination, colours and the vowels of the English alphabet. One lady quoted by Galton sees A as pure white, E as red, I as gamboge, O as black, U as purple, and Y as a dingier colour than I; whereas her daughter (this lady writes) sees A as blue, E as white, I as black, O as whitey-brownish and U as opaque brown, but it is self-evident to any occultist that these people do not perceive these colours with the pineal gland, but merely by a process of imaginative association, as also those who "see" certain colours in connection with the days of the week.[39]

Cyril Scott treats the matter with characteristic oversimplification. He probably did not realize, any more than Hargrave Jennings did, that the sevenfold division of the color spectrum is a modern and exclusively Western invention,[40] nor did he consider whether a Chinese- or Swahili-speaking psychic (for instance) would perceive exactly seven vowels. Sad to say, the study of tables of correspondences is a road that easily leads to skepticism. It always seems to be the case that "my" version comes through the pineal eye, whereas "yours" is merely elementary clairvoyance tainted by your imagination! This is not to dismiss a fundamental Hermetic principle; it is only to warn against putting too much faith in those who have limited it by imposing the boundaries of their own imagination, of their own alphabet, musical scale, or color-system.

SIX

Ancient Vowel-Songs

All this would be of merely theoretical interest were it not for the work of Charles-Emile Ruelle (1833–1912), the French philologist on whose history of the subject I have gratefully relied. Ruelle was a pupil of A. J. H. Vincent (1797–1868), a distinguished academician, and it must have been from Vincent that he conceived his interest in this matter and his determination to settle it once and for all. Vincent had in 1859 announced his discovery of a Greek vase in the Berlin museum that seemed to corroborate Demetrius's statement about the Egyptians singing a hymn of the vowels.[41] The vase depicted four musicians, two playing the cithara and two the double aulos. In five vertical columns ran a series of characters in which Vincent read the four archaic vowels A E I O, interpreting them without a doubt as musical notation. But Vincent had been snubbed by the aggressive François Joseph Fétis, uncrowned king of musicology, who saw no such thing in these indecipherable characters, and after a brief polemic the matter rested there.

When in 1865 Gustav Friedrich Parthey published the contents of two Graeco-Coptic magical papyri dating from between the fourth and seventh century C.E.,[42] it became apparent that the vowel-sequences were not isolated phenomena found on a few gems or artifacts, but that they were inserted with striking and disconcerting effect in otherwise legible Greek texts. Parthey did not for a moment doubt the musical character of these vowels, though he did not try to transcribe them into notation. The evidence became overwhelming in 1887, when Conrad Leemans published the great Leiden magical papyrus, which was full of such vowel-sequences, and the matter cried out for solution. Ruelle immediately went to work on the subject, and the following year brought out his first study.[43]

Although he had translated Nicomachus's book on music into French, Ruelle apparently did not trust himself with the actual transcription of these vowels into modern notation. For this task he engaged a series of collaborators, who seem to have been under an evil star: the first, Adolphe Populus, fell ill and died, and his appointed successor R. -J. Pottier did not even live long enough to start work on it. The transcription was eventually carried out by Elie Poirée, librarian at the Bibliothèque Sainte-Geneviève in Paris, and the results were published in 1900 at an international musicological congress.[44]

Ruelle favors the scheme of vowel-tone correspondence Moon high (p. 29). It makes no difference that he transposes it to the scale D C B♭ A G F E, for Greek pitches were relative ones, not fixed as ours are today. Applying this to the magical invocations, he and Poirée produce melodies such as this one, a transcription of the ninety-voweled amulet published by Kopp:

Example 3: The ninety-vowel incantation, interpreted by Ruelle

The opening phrase ι ε ο υ ω η, Poirée tells us, is a sequence
found repeatedly in the manuscripts. (The Miletus inscription also
began ι ε ο υ α η ω.) This is sufficient to indicate that the vowels
were not randomly chosen. Moreover, the first phrase is a palin-
drome (the first 17 notes reading the same backwards as forwards),
as are many other examples of what I cannot resist calling this
"gnostic, illicit song." There is evidently some definite rule behind
their composition, which is not to say a necessarily musical one.

The Oxford musicologist and composer Egon Wellesz, an
expert on the Byzantine domain, pooh-poohed Ruelle's and Poirée's
idea, saying that the vowels were symbols not of audible tones but
of the divine numbers, and that when transcribed they make
nonsense. "In fact, these melismata are so different from anything
we should expect that it is difficult to see how anyone could have
thought of accepting the transcriptions [of Ruelle and Poirée] as a
basis for further discussion."[45] A composer in twelve-tone style
who makes such remarks risks damage to his own glasshouse, but
the reader must judge whether there is any plausibility in the
Frenchmen's proposal. The recent publication of the Greek Magical
Papyri in English translation[46] makes it simple for anyone who
wants to follow their lead in finding a musical meaning to the
hundreds of vowel-sequences found therein; and future researchers
may come closer to the true reading of this repertory.

Another source, unknown to earlier scholars, is *The Discourse
on the Eighth and Ninth* from the library discovered at Nag
Hammadi. This is a discourse between Hermes Trismegistus and
his pupil concerning the soul's attainment of the eighth and ninth
spheres. It relates on the one hand to the treatises of the *Corpus
Hermeticum*, and on the other to the Greek magical papyri of the
same period (early centuries C.E.), for it includes two sequences of
untranslatable vowels. The second of these is explicitly presented
as a hymn, which tends to support Ruelle's theory that the vowels
have a musical meaning.

O grace! After these things I give thanks by singing a hymn to
thee. For I have received life from thee when thou madest me
wise. I praise thee. I call thy name that is hidden within me: α ω

εε ω ηηη ωωω ιιι ωωωω οοοοο ωωωωω υυυυυυ
ωωωωωωωωωωωωωωωωωωωωωωωωω. Thou art the one who exists with
the spirit. I sing a hymn to thee reverently.[47]

This "hymn" would sound as follows when transcribed in the
three musical systems proposed previously:

Example 4.i: Nag Hammadi incantation, interpreted in "Moon low" system

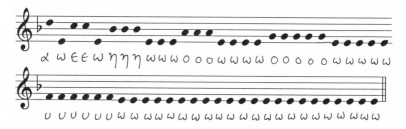

Example 4.ii: "Moon high" system

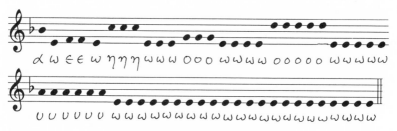

Example 4.iii: "Phoenician" system

But it is naive to suppose that vowel-songs can only be rendered in the Dorian mode, and in the diatonic genus. That is only one of the twenty-one combinations offered by the Greek musical system, which has seven different modes or octave-species (the sequences from B-B, C-C, D-D, E-E, F-F, G-G, and A-A), each one susceptible to performance in three different genera (diatonic, chromatic, and enharmonic). Multiplied by the three systems we have listed, this would give sixty-three possible ways of transcribing any vowel-sequence into music. Some of these would produce a very different kind of chant. We return to the opening of the ninety-vowel incantation (Example 1) in order to illustrate some different modal and generic interpretations of the seven tones.

Example 5.i: Moon low, Phrygian mode, diatonic genus

Example 5.ii: Phoenician system, Dorian mode, chromatic genus

Example 5.iii: Moon high, Lydian mode, enharmonic genus

It is certainly an attractive idea, that the vowel-sequences encode a secret song. But if this is so, then it must be said that the Greeks nowhere else chose to notate their music in this clever and convenient way; and that even if this was an exception, it is very unlikely that any modern readings agree with ancient practice. As is often the case with research into ancient occultism, the enterprise reveals far more about the researchers than about the subject. And this is as it should be, for such research is primarily of value for the spiritual journey it affords to the seeker; almost never is it of any importance to the general or even the learned public. In confirmation of this priniciple, the enterprises described in the next chapter have almost nothing to teach about Antiquity, but everything to do with the spiritual concerns of modern times.

SEVEN

Modern Vowel-Songs

By the last decade of the nineteenth century, the song of the vowels was in the air. There is no need to presume classical learning or occult intentions on the part of those who incorporated them into musical settings, but it is noticeable that they made their appearance at a time when Hermetists and Theosophists were educating a wider public about the doctrine of correspondences, the reality of the planetary energies, and the harmony of the spheres.

Richard Wagner was very likely behind it all, setting an example by the wordless songs he gave to the Rhine Maidens, the Valkyries, and the Flower Maidens of *Parsifal*—all beings not of this world. The French experimental theater of the 1890s was inspired by Wagner's innovations at the Festival Theater of Bayreuth and, like the German master's work, it trod a fine line between art and religion. One result was a multi-media *Song of Songs*, presented on 11 December 1891 by Paul-Napoléon Roinard. This specimen of "total art" was subtitled "Symphony of Spiritual Love, in eight mystic emblems and three paraphrases, with music." Each of the tableaux had its dominant vowels and its particular color, tonality, and perfume. In the first, for instance, the recitation was dominated by the vowels I and O, the music was in D major, the stage decorations were of a bright orange color, and the hall was perfumed with the scent of violets.[48] There was an uproarious response to this fusion of the arts, which offered everything the *fin-de-siècle* could desire: Wagner's *Gesamtkunstwerk*, the synaesthesia of Baudelaire (and of Huysmans' decadent hero Des Esseintes), with a *frisson* of erotic mysticism in the mode of the Sâr Peladan. It was like one of the Renaissance tables of correspondences brought to life, though to the worldly audience the association may have been more to the effects of hashish.

At this very moment, Claude Debussy, now returned from residence in Rome and frequenting esoteric circles in Paris, must have been preparing his three *Nocturnes* for orchestra, of which the third, *Sirènes*, features a wordless female choir. The piece was finished in 1892. The Sirens of Homer's *Odyssey* XII were the bird-bodied women whose song lured sailors to their death, but to the Neoplatonists they were a positive symbol of the lure of the soul's true home, attainable only at the sacrifice of the material body and its world. Debussy can never be suspected of naïvety in his approach to mythological images, and his music is the most persuasive witness to his familiarity with other worlds. Yet he missed here the golden opportunity to color the Sirens' song with the vowels that surely resound in those astral regions: an omission imaginatively rectified by the conductor Pierre Boulez, who in his performances and recordings of the *Nocturnes* has the singers vary the vowels to match the different orchestral sonorities. Here is the characteristic theme of the choir:

Example 6: Debussy

Without a doubt there were other instances in this period of composers writing vowel-music, but I have not been able to search for their forgotten scores. The American dancer Isidora Duncan apparently used such music in 1905 as the accompaniment to her enormously successful Paris recitals. In her manner of presentation, half veiled and accompanied by a concealed orchestra and a wordless choir, the critic Armande de Polignac saw the harbinger of the supreme art of the future, free from vulgarity and from any literary distractions. Mme. de Polignac mentions specifically that "These choirs or solo voices might sing with closed lips, or on one of the vowels, chosen according to its number of harmonics for the timbre or degree of intensity desired."[49] These are not the words of one ignorant of the subject.

The whole topic of vowel-songs now called forth its definitive treatment in a monograph by Edmond Bailly (1850–1916), a lovable bookseller and Theosophist, minor composer, poet, and scholar, whose shop near the Paris Opéra had been frequented by Debussy and Erik Satie in the 1890s. Bailly not only set out to collect all that seemed worth preserving of the history of the song of the vowels, but to recreate the song itself. His *Chant des Voyelles* for women's choir, flutes and harps was first performed in early June 1906, at the Theosophical Society's Congress in Paris, and repeated on other occasions.[50] The piece was published in 1912 by Bailly's own press, "L'Art Indépendant," in his book *Le Chant des Voyelles comme invocation aux dieux planétaires, suivi d'une restitution vocale avec accompagnement*. It is given entire in the Appendix.

The present book does not seek to make redundant this engaging production of Bailly's multiple talents: there are things of value therein which I have not borrowed, for each book has its own unity and reflects its own time. Bailly thought of his *Chant des Voyelles* not as a composition in the usual sense, but as a "veritable palingenesis of knowledge;" not the fruit of creative originality, but of viewing intuitively the indestructible screen of the past.[51] He defends at length his choice of notes, of instruments, of harmony, and discusses the proper incense with which to perfume the invocation (he favors the recipe given to Moses in Exodus 30:22-4). Bailly uses the same vowel-tone arrangement as Ruelle and Poirée (our system no. 2), but changes the vowel omega to OU in order to make it better distinguishable from the omicron. In point of fact, he does not pretend to definite knowledge of what the vowels should be, beyond the "ideal triad A, I, OU, prototype of every vocal system, whose simplest modulations complete the septenary."[52]

The key to Bailly's approach is that it was not a piece of classical antiquarianism, but an Egyptian magical rite that he sought to recreate, and this as a living and effective act. (He says that he has necessarily left in the dark certain truly Theosophical points of the subject.) One can well believe him when he adds that "a great impression was caused by the hearing of this mystical invocation in the presence of an élite audience of more than four hundred persons, gathered from every corner of the civilized world,"[53] so that they demanded a second performance at the close of the Congress.

Apart from this musical curiosity, the vowel-song most consistent with the theurgic purpose of the ancient chants is that of Alexander Scriabin. In his symphonic poem of 1910, *Prometheus* (*The Poem of Fire*), Scriabin gives the chorus the text E-A, O HO-A, O-HO. An ardent Theosophist, he would have found the word OEAOHOO in *The Secret Doctrine* of H. P. Blavatsky,[54] where it occurs in the "Stanzas of Dzyan." The passage in question reads: "The Root remains, the Light remains, the Curds remain, and still OEAOHOO is one." (Stanza 3:5). Blavatsky explains that OEAOHOO signifies "Father-Mother of the Gods," or "the Six in One," or "the Septenary Root from which all proceeds." Scriabin's writings emphasized the divine nature of the human being, while his personal philosophy endowed him with a central, "Promethean" rôle in human evolution;[55] so it is not difficult to see why the symphonic poem, which is in a way a self-portrait of the composer, bears the imprint or incarnation in sound of the cosmocratic name.

Example 7: Scriabin

A few other eminent composers were also tempted by the atmospheric effect of wordless song. Ravel's ballet of Greek mythology *Daphnis and Chloë* (1909–11) uses a choir of mixed voices behind the scene, directing them to sing only with mouths closed or open. Their presence is most keenly felt, perhaps, at the climax of the third scene, which depicts a sunrise as no other composer has done, before or since. In their ecstatic greeting to Apollo, we surely hear an echo, transformed by its passage through space and time, of the planetary hymns of Egypt and Atlantis:

Example 8: Ravel

Like his master Debussy, Gustav Holst neglected the opportunity to exploit the colors of different vowels in his impressionistic suite *The Planets* (1915). In the last movement, "Neptune, the Mystic," he introduces a six-part female choir, also placed offstage, singing "to the vowel *u* as in *sun*." Their unaccompanied chant ends the work, repeated to inaudibility in order to give an impression of timelessness, or of the infinite distances beyond the solar system.[56] (See Example 9, p. 54.)

After World War I, such Romantic yearnings were exhausted; there was little room for Sirens in the world of *neue Sachlichkeit*. They returned in 1967 in an epoch-making work: Karlheinz Stockhausen's religio-erotic *Stimmung* for six voices. It was here that Stockhausen, after making his reputation as a composer in the avant-garde style of serial atonality, returned to the roots of harmony. The hour-long piece is based on a single chord, B^b f b^b d' a^b c"; in other words, on harmonics 2, 3, 4, 5, 7, and 9 of an absent fundamental B^b_1. The voices sing not only these tones, however, but are instructed to emphasize specific harmonics of them, achieved through use of specific vowels (see the fifth exercise in Chapter 10). With prophetic insight, Stockhausen recreated a song of the vowels for our time, and gave to the voices, as text, none other than the names of the Gods, drawn from every religion.

This bar is to be
repeated until the
sound is lost in
the distance.

Example 9: Holst

It was partly the example of *Stimmung* and partly the UNESCO
recordings of Tibetan Buddhist and Bön chants that kindled a new
interest in vowel-song and vocal harmonics during the 1970s.
David Hykes was a pioneer in this, founding the Harmonic Choir,
training them in unfamiliar vocal techniques, and composing
music for them to sing, with its fullest effect in resonant church
buildings such as the Abbey of Thoronet in Southern France and the

Cathedral of Saint John the Divine in New York City. Thus many listeners have been permitted to share Sir Richard Paget's ecclesiastical initiation into the harmonic mysteries of the vowels. And in David Hykes's solo song, heard at the beginning of Peter Brook's film about Gurdjieff, *Meetings with Remarkable Men*, this sound has reached a wider audience still. Then, during the 1980s, Jill Purce, an English expert in both Tibetan and Western techniques, gave workshops and demonstrations in many countries, setting hundreds of others on the path of discovery and practice. Other experimenters are legion, especially now that the digital analysis and computerized synthesis of vowel-sounds is such a lively field. In fact, the reawakened awareness of harmonics is perhaps the most significant musical development of the post-modern period, for it marks the re-establishment of music in its eternal and natural principles.

EIGHT

The Names of the Gods

In the previous chapter I singled out Karlheinz Stockhausen, David Hykes, and Jill Purce from the many recent explorers of vowels and harmonics, because they have made explicit the sacred quality of this phenomenon: Stockhausen, by setting specifically the names of gods; Hykes, by the devotional atmosphere with which he surrounds his performances; Purce, by the direct connections she makes between this kind of singing and Tibetan esoteric practice. There is something about vowel-song that makes it, as Demetrius noted, most suitable for hymns to the gods.

One reason for this is that the gods themselves often have names consisting purely of vowels. The best known example is the Tetragrammaton ה ו ה י, the four-lettered name of the God of Moses, revealed at the Burning Bush (Exodus 3:15). This name is never pronounced by pious Jews,[57] being replaced whenever it occurs in the scriptures by the word *Adonai*, meaning "Lord." The Vulgate represents it by "Dominus," and most English bibles by "LORD" in capitals.

The letters of the Tetragrammaton, iod-he-vau-he, are variously transliterated: JHVH, YHWH, IEVE, Iahve, etc. It is commonly said that the Hebrew alphabet has no vowels, and that these have to be supplied either through knowledge of the words or else indicated by the "Masoretic points" written around the alphabetical letters. But no one could deny that aleph and iod, at the very least, are vowels. Fabre d'Olivet, who learned his Hebrew from an Egyptian colleague, Elias Boctor, came to the conclusion that the consonantal nature of the Hebrew alphabet was a misunderstanding: that the language derived from Egyptian, its alphabet from that of the Chaldaeans, and that it includes seven vowels:

> Aleph: soft vowel, represented by â
> Heh: stronger vowel, represented by è, h
> Cheth: very strong pectoral vowel,
> represented by è, ẖ, c̓h
> Vav with point *hirek*: obscure, enclosed vowel,
> represented by ou, u, y
> Vav with point *holem*: brilliant vowel,
> represented by o
> Iod: hard vowel, represented by î
> Ain: deep, guttural vowel, represented by ẖo, wẖo

—to which Fabre d'Olivet adds an eighth "implied consonantal vowel" of varying value. Following his interpretation, the Tetragrammaton would be a true vowel-name, which Fabre d'Olivet spells Ihôah and translates as "the-Being-who-is-who-was-and-who-will-be."[58] Its pronunciation would approximate to "*ieoue.*"

Another ancient vowel-name is Iaô (Ιαω), frequently found on Gnostic gems and mentioned in Macrobius's *Saturnalia* as a name of the Sun God.[59] The Abbé Barthélemy, in his study of Egyptian medals mentioned in Chapter 3, notes that the name is often combined with depictions of Harpocrates, child-god of the winter solstice. He suggests that since the vowel iota corresponds to the Sun, and alpha and omega are the first and last letters of the Greek alphabet, Iaô could mean: "The Sun, beginning and end of all things." In a more profound sense, he goes on, the Pythagoreans may have enclosed in this brief formula of beginning, middle and end their ideas of the universe and of the Supreme Being. As shown in Chapter 1, these are the three vowels most appropriate for fixing the physical limits of the system, and hence most appropriate as symbols of completeness.

Diodorus Siculus (1st century B.C.E.) says expressly that Moses received his laws from the god called Iaô, and it is the consensus of modern scholars that this name replaced the Tetragrammaton after the latter ceased to be pronounced by Jews. From the Gentile point of view, Iahve and Iaô were among the multitude of names for the supreme or solar deity. The symbolic events surrounding the nativity of Jesus, in turn, identify him as another avatar of the child-god of the winter solstice, while his biography, whatever its historical basis, replicates that of every solar god or hero. So is Iaô the same as the god of Moses, the same as Jesus Christ, and are all three emblematic of the Sun? Paul-Ernest Jablonski, in *Pantheon Aegyptiorum* (1750), rejected the first pairing: on etymological grounds, he could not equate Iaô with Iahve. But he did not hesitate to identify Iaô as a pagan adumbration of Christ. Jablonski explains that the sun in question is the spiritual, not the material sun, hence the attribute is applicable to Jesus as the Light of the World.[60]

These brief parallels between the Abrahamic religions and paganism introduce us to the tangle of interlocking symbols and deities which Pico della Mirandola was perhaps the first to attempt to unravel, in the late fifteenth century. Athanasius Kircher took Pico's work considerably further in his *Oedipus Aegyptiacus* of 1650, although since he was a Jesuit and all his work carried the imprimatur of the Catholic Church, he trod very carefully whenever he approached the holy ground of Christianity. In the age of Enlightenment, with the waning of sacerdotal censorship, the objective study of comparative religion at last became feasible in a few . countries, notably France. Charles Dupuis (1742–1809), in his *L'Origine de tous les Cultes* (3 volumes, 1795), set himself the goal of proving that all ancient mythology and symbolism referred to the annual journey of the Sun, hence that it was all a relic of mankind's original solar cult. In particular, Dupuis applied the solar myth to elucidate the Twelve Labors of Hercules and the Voyage of the Argonauts—then proceeded to treat in just the same way the life of Jesus. The work unleashed a storm of controversy, and it doubtless did overstate its case. Nevertheless, it opened the field for the non-confessional treatment of the Jewish and Christian religions.

In the English-speaking world, the primary monument to this kind of research is the *Anacalypsis* of Godfrey Higgins (1771–1833), with its prefatory volume *The Celtic Druids*, in which are found many pages on the equivalence of ancient vowel-names. Higgins was an admirer of Dupuis' work, but not limited (or, perhaps, not controlled) by the rational philosophy of the Frenchman. In various parts of *Anacalypsis* he juxtaposes the following names, with the implication that they should be regarded as virtual identities:

(1) The one-lettered name I as denoting the sacred island of IHVH, ultimately reducible to his first letter.[61]

(2) The two-lettered name IE, equally referring to "the self-existing Jah or Jehovah" (cf. Psalm 68:4 in the English Psalter which names God as "JAH"). This name also appears as the EI on the sanctuary of Apollo at Delphi. Early Greek writing, Higgins explains, could read from right to left, hence the EI is indeed IE[62]—and by implication IHVH is the Sun God.

(3) The three-lettered name IAO, which the Greeks considered to be the name of the Jewish God. In Hebrew it is the letters iod-he-vau.

(4) The Tetragrammaton iod-he-vau-he, which the ancients wrote and pronounced variously JAHO, JEVO, and sometimes IAOU, is IAO or IEU plus the definite article. This is none other than the *Juve* of the Etruscans, from which the Romans took their *Jove; Jupiter* then being of the same family, with *piter,* "father," added. The same name is heard in India, where the devotees of Krishna sing "JEYE! JEYE!"

(5) The name JEHOVA or JEHOVAH. This is generally explained as deriving from the Tetragrammaton, made pronounceable by interspersing the Masoretic vowel-points from *Adonai:* thus JeHoVaH. We have already heard Eusebius say that the Jews expressed the name of God with the seven vowels. Higgins also quotes scholars who suggest that the Bacchantes' cry "EVOHE!" derived from the very same word.[63]

The scattered suggestions in Higgins's work are pulled together expertly in this passage from the Theosophist and Gnostic scholar, G. R. S. Mead (1863–1933):

I would suggest that Ieou is a transliteration of the four-lettered mystery name of the creator according to Semitic and Chaldaean tradition, the tetragrammaton of the Kabalah. Theodoret tells us that the Samaritans pronounced this name Iabe (Iave) and the Jews Iaô. Since the sixteenth century, by adding the vowels of

Adonai to the unpronounceable Y H V H, it has been pronounced Jehovah. It is now generally written Yahweh; but there is no certainty in the matter, beyond the fact that Jehovah is absolutely wrong. Ieou or Iaô are probably atttempts in Greek transliteration at the same Semitic name, which contained letters totally unrepresentable in Greek: Yahoo or Yahuwh perchance, the name hidden in Iacchus (Yach), still further corrupted into Bacchus by the Greeks. Iacchus was the mystery-name of the creative power in that great mystery tradition; Bacchus was the name in the popular cult.[64]

Mead's observations are highly suggestive. It seems that there was a sacred name consisting in the vowel-sequence that begins with the high sound of see, moves through the intermediate late or far, and ends with the deep vowel go or you; and that this name, in its variant forms, was applied to the highest of the gods, whichever that might be. The name in its fullest form embraces both sides of the vowel-pyramid, covering the range to which classical authors subsequently assigned the seven notes of the scale. Moreover, it denotes the supreme God whose power includes those of all the lesser gods. In the purest Hebrew monotheism, of course, these other gods are not permitted to exist, since Iahve is the one and only power in the universe. But if this vowel-name is that of the Sun God, then the powers he includes are those of the other planets, as we mentioned in connection with Apollo in Chapter 3. This furnishes the name with its astral dimension, also expressed in musical notes as the Harmony of the Spheres.

A disagreeable but intriguing sidelight on the subject of Iaô comes from Jean Robin, the author of two books on René Guénon. Here is an extract from an essay on "Seth, the unknown god," in which Robin discusses the cult of Seth-Typhon, the god who murdered Osiris in the Egyptian myth of death and resurrection:[65]

In a fairly late Gnostic complex, Seth, who had now become the god of magicians, was invoked under the name of *Io*, which is Egyptian for "ass," or *Iao*, the cock-headed divinity. Through the closeness of this *Io* or *Iao* to *Iahve*, Seth was soon assimilated to the God of the Jews, who were reproached by the lower classes, and very naturally so, as allies of the Hyksos [the "Shepherd Kings," invaders of Egypt]. But the dizzying thought occurs to us that here is a dress rehearsal, as it were, which imputes deicide— here the murder of Osiris—to a scapegoat associated with Judaism. And according to a seriously grounded tradition, the antisemitism of the Egyptian plebians communicated itself, like the plague, to the Greeks and Romans, who are known to have accused the first Christians of worshipping "the god with an ass's head."

It is not for me to unravel the biblical Seth from the Egyptian one, nor to comment on late Gnostic texts (rich in vowel incantations, by the way) such as the Coptic *Gospel of the Egyptians* in the Nag Hammadi collection, where Seth comes down from heaven and puts on Jesus as a garment, for the salvation of his children.[66] Yet I will add, in all seriousness, that no animal would have served better as a hidden symbol of Iaô than the patient and unmusical ass, which cries as best it can the name of the Unknown God. What else can one imagine the ecstatic invocations of the Bacchics to have sounded like?

None of the authors mentioned in this chapter approached this subject with any awareness of its musical dimension. In Higgins's great synthesis, music is conspicuously absent, neither did it interest any of the Continental scholars of comparative religion, with the exceptions of Fabre d'Olivet and Albert von Thimus.[67] Later, the Kabbalistic scholar Paul Vulliaud (1875–1950) surmised that "music," in primitive times, must have meant much more than it does today, being a term for a "cosmosophic" knowledge given only to initiates.[68] The very word "music," he says, signifies to penetrate or to initiate into mysteries; for example, Philo Judaeus describes Moses as initiated into the *music* of the Egyptians. In antiquity, Vulliaud goes on, the universe was imagined with nine spheres, sounding seven tones (Mercury and Venus shared one, and the Earth was silent) corresponding to seven vowels. Vulliaud defines thus the chord of these vowels or tones: "*La Parole, le Verbe, en un mot* that Divinity who by the organ of

Apollo is the imperishable Heptachord, regulates the melodious concert of the celestial movements."[69] Thus he sidesteps the difficult issue of the vowels as acoustical entities, reducing their "music" to a metaphor. This will always be the case, it seems, when precise musical knowledge is lacking.

Although we have not yet learned anything musical about these names, we can penetrate further into the astral theology behind them. Here is an elucidation from another of those scholars who spent their lives in search of mankind's original language and Ur-religion, Adolphe Lethierry-Barrois (died 1863). These words are the opening of his posthumous *Hébreu Primitif*:[70]

> The Hebrew letters are the ciphers or signs of the zodiac, from which the words of the Hebrew language itself are formed; the consonants are the letters or ciphers which assemble around the vowels to form the words, just as the constellations assemble around the Sun, image of the Divinity, and compose the community of stars over which it presides. The constellations of the Zodiac formed the twelve great gods of Graeco-Roman antiquity, corresponding to the twelve stations of the Sun, and these constellations were distinguished by the letters from Aleph to Thau; attributes or energies of the same divinity, they are so to speak the pearls which have formed the necklace of the Zodiac, and the vowels corresponding to the seven planets which surround the Sun are the voices which give sound or color to the consonants; they form the word, and the word is the Divinity itself. The priests of Abydos would recite the mystic hymn of the seven vowels, or the name of Jehovah which unites them. It is through the word or Son of God that all creation was made, for the voice and the vowel give life to the consonants, just as the Sun gives color to bodies, to matter; and the consonants or radical letters, animated by the vowels, form the roots that compose the primitive, monosyllabic language, just as the *koua* contain the system of the Chinese language.

Lethierry-Barrois does not specify what these seven vowels are. When he comes to give the Hebrew letters corresponding to the signs of the Zodiac, he simply begins with Aleph and proceeds alphabetically, never reaching the twenty-second letter, Thau. The value of his explanation is more metaphysical than philological, for he makes a telling parallel between the workings of astrology and those of the alphabet. The consonants, like the signs of the Zodiac, are as it were static moulds into which the vowels or planets, by their movement in time, infuse life. The invocation by vowels is therefore to be read as an affirmation of these seven dynamic powers.

I turn now to a more detailed analysis of the sacred names, letter by letter, which is highly speculative. The author is Adolphe Bertet (1812–1875), who wrote under the pseudonym of "Le Paysan de Saint Pierre" ("Saint Peter's Peasant").[71] In the course of a digression on correspondences, he explains some of the theories of planetary music (which he transcribes into a sort of waltz), and then says:

> The heavens have given us not only music, but also writing: it was Apollo, it was Orpheus, who taught music to the Greeks; it was Cadmus, or the serpentine one, who taught them writing; it was the jealous God who taught the art of writing to Moses, by engraving with his own hand the Decalogue on the stone tables on Mount Horeb, in the desert of Sinai. (Exod. 24:12)
>
> Let us ask what this writing is, that is understood, in all languages without distinction, by those who have received its key by means of initiation into the secret doctrines, and we will understand thereby what the so-called "gift of tongues" is, bestowed on the apostles by the Holy Spirit and promised to all the faithful, as a blessing of confirmation or initiation into exclusive mysteries.
>
> Each of the planets is magically denoted by just one of these letters: the moon by A, Mercury by E, Venus by H, the Sun by J, Mars by O, Jupiter by Y, Saturn by U or the long Greek O. These are the letters that the gods taught to men, or, in other words, that the cabalistic priests attributed to the gods.

Bertet goes on to give precise meanings to the vowels, and to deduce from them the significances of sacred words or formulae, which I summarize as follows:[72]

J or Jod is the sign of the Sun or of the God of Light, and its meaning is the light of truth or knowledge.

E or He is Mercury, messenger and hence priest of the Sun.

O or Omega [also U] is Saturn or Time, which was the true god of the Jews.

V or Vau is the Morning-star, the number 5, which expresses the domination of intelligence over matter; also, communication between the material and the spiritual worlds.

A or Alpha is the Moon, the Mother, emblem of the Mysteries, thus representing gnosis, the church, or sacred science.

Thus equipped, Bertet can read the sacred names like a book. JHEOVA or JOHEVAH (יהΩιA) means the *light* of truth or knowledge, manifesting through the *priesthood*, in *time*, under the emblem of the *mysteries*.

JAO ('ΑΩ), the Savior of the Gnostics, is a name made from the sign of the Sun, that of the Moon, and that of Saturn or Time. Thus it signifies the *light* of truth, manifesting under the emblem of the *mysteries* in *time*.

The JUPITER of the Philosophers is *piter* (father), the universal creative force, manifesting in *time* through its first-born son, the *Sun*.

The EI placed in a circle on the temple of Apollo at Delphi signifies the emblem of unity or harmony, enclosing the messenger or *priest* of the *Sun*. The priesthood thereby asserted its union with God, arrogating to itself (and here Bertet's true theme emerges) the honors that belong to God alone. For Bertet, far from being sympathetic to this kind of doctrine, is only writing about it in order to illustrate the mystery-mongering of the ancient priests, and the folly of those who attribute an interest in such trivia to the One God.

Finally he explains All-El-Uia as composed of:

A, the beginning, the first of the seven heavens; the Moon.

J, the Sun, the middle heaven or mediator.

U, the end or the last heaven, that of Saturn; the Hebraic definition of God himself.

El, an abbreviation of Eloïm, the gods or second causes.

All or Alla, God in the singular, Sabaoth, the leader of the celestial host, the supreme god of the Jews.

The exclamation ALLELUIA thus translates as "O *God* supreme, and you second causes or *gods, beginning, middle,* and *end* of all, be blessed and glorified on Earth as in Heaven!"

This, says our Peasant, is "the language which is understood in every tongue, and it is the communication of this key that is veiled under the fable of the gift of tongues communicated by the Holy Spirit in the true confirmation or initiation into the last, reserved mysteries."[73]

Bertet is ingenious, but not, one feels, endowed with real esoteric knowledge of this subject. It is a different matter when one turns to H. P. Blavatsky (1831–1891), who, writing in English, put the idea of the seven sacred vowels into far wider currency than it had ever had before. In Chapter 7 there was mention of the word OEAOHOO, adapted by Scriabin, which occurs in the "Stanzas of Dzyan." These stanzas of Tibetan provenance are the text on which *The Secret Doctrine* (1888) is a commentary. Concerning OEAOHOO, Blavatsky says in that work that "all depends upon the accent given to these seven vowels, which may be pronounced as ONE, three, or even seven syllables, by adding an '*e*' after the final '*o*'. This mystic name is given out, because without a thorough mastery of the triple pronunciation it remains for ever ineffectual."[74]

Later, Blavatsky distinguishes between the different versions of the name: "The names answering to Parabrahman, to Brahma, and Manu, the first *thinking* Man, are composed of one-vowelled, three-vowelled and seven-vowelled sounds."[75] Briefly, Parabrahman is the Absolute, Brahma the creator God, and Manu the integral, seven-principled human being. Echoes of these names occur, perhaps, in the pure "Ah" pronounced as a mantram in Tibetan Tantrism; in the three-lettered Iaô, which we have seen applied to the Sun God and to the Jewish Creator; and in the full sequence of seven vowels which the Greek alphabet may have been formed to express. Concerning the latter, Blavatsky, no doubt steered by her secretary G. R. S. Mead through the Gnostic and Hermetic literature which he knew so well, calls attention to the equivalence of the seven vowels—or "Seven Voices," as Mead translates them[76]—with the "Seven Zones of *post mortem* ascent, in the Hermetic writings, in each of which the 'Mortal' leaves one of his 'Souls,' or Principles; until arrived on the plane above all Zones, he remains as the great Formless Serpent of Absolute Wisdom, or the Deity Itself."[77]

NINE

Egyptian Mysteries

We have come to the core of our subject, to the deeper mysteries of the vowels that have given these far-flown theories their life and their perennial fascination. One cannot really believe that the hierophants of theocratic Egypt were content merely to mouth vowel-songs to the seven planetary gods, as Christian congregations sing hymns to the Holy Trinity. Egyptian religion, at least before the decadent times that constitute practically all of recorded history, was not merely a hopeful gesture towards an unknown power, nor was it a sacerdotal plot for keeping the people in superstitious subjection, though like every religion it may at times have sunk to that. It was a theurgic art, or science, conducted with definite aims in view and achieving definite effects, and this during a period of at least the ten thousand years that Plato allows to the theocratic civilization of Egypt.

Having said as much, it is time to leave erudition behind, and to put the critical faculty in abeyance, becoming instead a vehicle for ideas that seem to have a ring of authenticity about them. The reader will concede that they are, at the very least, poetic.

Among the most important works of Egyptian theurgy was the manipulation of the forces of life and death, which this people understood better than any subsequent civilization except the Tibetan. Definite techniques were used to help people through the process of dying and to procure for them favorable conditions in the after-death state. This was possible through a thorough understanding of the several principles of the human being, which cohere during waking life but suffer a separation at death that may well be traumatic if suitable preparations have not been made. The philosophers tell us, and rightly so, that the best preparation for death is a virtuous life—but the Egyptians went beyond that. In the case of adepts, among whom in the earlier period were numbered the Pharaohs or divine priest-kings, steps were taken to arrest the normal process of dissolution. One of these was the mummification of the physical body, which had the effect of preventing the transmigration of the soul into another body, so long as the mummy remained intact. More important still was the ritual which caused the Pharaoh's astral body also to resist what is sometimes called the "second death," so that his personality could remain indefinitely intact. The purpose of this extraordinary practice was to keep the beneficent influences of the adept-king's consciousness in Egypt, to the advantage of the whole civilization and presumably with the consent of the Pharaoh himself.[78]

The method of this enchantment was a musical ritual:

> The seven strings of the magic lyre gave out, as they sounded, vibratory numbers corresponding to the astral waves of the seven planets. The Hierophant applied, for his musical purposes, the mechanism of the cosmic vibrations, and it was thus that at the propitious moment, he proceeded to the animation of the transvitalized phantasm of the Pharaoh.
>
> To capture the astral influx of planetary life, and to transfuse it into the mummy, the Hierophant made the seven notes resonate magically: A, G, F, E, D, C, B; according to a slurred ternary rhythm which repeated like a charmed circle.
>
> Then the atmosphere of the tomb was animated by lines of subtle energies, and the prodigy of an extraordinary condensation of cosmic life manifested by the rhythmic palpitations of the supervitalized air.
>
> The astral waves became more and more condensed, so as to form a wondrous fluidic spiral, the shape of the magic vortex of protection and animation whose center was the mummy itself.
>
> At that instant, the Hierophant intoned the incantation of astral life and fixed it, following the law of magical correspondences, in the breast of the mummy, whose phantasm was

animated by an inextinguishable flame: and the miraculous existence of the Pharaoh's double would last as long as the land of Egypt.[79]

The author of this passage, Fidèle Amy-Sage, adds parenthetically that if the mummy should ever be disturbed, as in the case of Tutankhamen, the spell would break.

The supernatural power of the seven notes intoned by the Hierophant derives from their ability to touch off correspondences on other levels than the physical. At their highest, they are a distant echo of the vowels which sounded forth in the sevenfold laughter of the Creator God,[80] and became the "Seven Spirits before the Throne" of the Apocalypse with their Seven Thunders, Voices, or Vowels. In the solar system, they are reflected as the characteristic vibrations of the seven planets which control individual destiny, as well as the forces that hold together both planets and atomic particles. In former times, when the world was ruled by the wise, the secrets of activating these energies acoustically were known and put to use. Among the material witnesses to their powers are certain of the great stone monuments—far older than archeologists are eager to admit—which legend tells us were built, like the mythical walls of Thebes, with the use of sound. The music we hear today no longer works in this way, because the keys to the laws of correspondence are lost, or hidden; also because our world has become, in a way, too solid for its secret resonances to be sprung into action.[81] Our age is a darker one, and this being so, the loss of music's power over matter is providential, removing one more source of energy that would have surely have been abused. Also we are subjected to temporal and spiritual leaders who would, on the whole, be more of a liability than a blessing to humanity if their astral influences were not promptly dissolved after their deaths.

Still, the human being is always a microcosm in potential, and the sevenfold archetype exists in us, imprinted—if one likes the Hermetic imagery—on our souls during our downward journey from the beatific Eighth Sphere into earthly incarnation. It is only by the awakening of our own microcosmic nature (the Platonic "remembrance") that we can achieve any understanding of the macrocosm; for as we can know nothing but our own states, it is our nature that dictates the sort of world that we are capable of projecting, and receiving. A creature that is not a microcosm, like an animal, has correspondingly less chance of understanding the greater world.

The search for understanding, hampered as it is by the conditions of our present incarnation, may find a more congenial climate in the halls of the after-life, even though the opportunities to act on that understanding may be lacking there. So, at least, the Egyptians were led to believe. In one hall in particular, the knowledge to be gained takes a musical form:

> The Third Gate. Received by the Harpist of the Gate, the Adept has entered, by the virtue of music, into the domain of spiritual festivals. And at once the murmur arises from the ocean of tones, and the fleshless, boneless spooks flee away, transparent alchemists that they are.
>
> The melodious welcome of the Master of the Harp is able to retain for an instant, through the three dimensions of sonority and the translucency of expressive modulation, the spirit of the "one clothed in linen," and now invites it to "pass a blessed day here."
>
> He even presses it, insisting: "There is song and music for the spirit of your ears. Pass a blessed day here, pass a blessed day."
>
> And now indeed the hero allows himself to be persuaded. In so doing, he attains sublimity, through the language of the singing soul whose voice expands in the interior world.
>
> At first a simple interlude, this musical intervention of the Harpist of the Gate has transmuted spoken language into song. The melodious sound thus reinforces the magical power of the Word—that Word which can create the Universe by the simple emission of vowels, without even the help of articulated words.
>
> Once arrived at this stage, the Adept enters of his own volition into his proper circuit. By a kind of current of self-induction, of magnetism in the closed circle traced by his own will, he becomes his own lodestone. From henceforth, he can go his own way free from malevolent Destiny, "passing blessed days" for ever after.

Truly, as soon as the Third Gate is opened before his eyes, being the gate of Intellect, the judges pass into the background, to the invisible ranks. Thus the spiritual sight of the Adept can be lifted up to the Gardens of Enchantment, to the depths of the groves where is hidden the hieroglyph of the greater god which is Number, creator of harmony.

And here is a magic whose fragrances liberate the initiated hero's soul from all the bonds accumulated by reason. It ransacks reason and inertia, to leave in its place, in his heart, nothing besides Love.

An abyss thousands of years deep engulfs all visible materiality in the impalpable realm of sound; it heaves up the immortal spirit, only to plunge it into a fatality of delight.

Now an invincible element, he approaches the meadows of dream, the ladders of incense, the glades of the Western constellations, the blessed fields of beans in flower, in the dew of the world's first dawnings. He is on the peaks. He is in the empire of ecstasy. All is clear: the Idea is diamantine.

Before the eyes of his spirit, the hieroglyphic alphabet of the Intelligible World scintillates in scattered stars against the crystal horizons. The fragrances of music are columns of magic smoke. A young lake of perfumes, blossoming with water-lilies, rises out of the subterranean night and becomes for him the whole sea.

And here a note springs forth in purity from the invisible sources of the land of life. It is the fountain of the Infinite. It is a new language. Like the light, it is the daughter of the breath which gave it birth.

But leaning close to him appeared the face of the "Beloved": a divine being, having in herself the gifts of expression and of silence—even more expressive by silences than by tones or accents, more lively in rhythms and syncopations than in ornaments and grace-notes, more moving by subtle modes than by sheer power.

She it is whom the great initiates, the highest adepts, have named "The Divine Mother of Silence." The only name, a truly wondrous one, that suits this goddess is: Harmony.

Now he knows that in the great adventure of real and fictive life, the drama is Love, and the goal is Harmony. To break the Harmony or to sin against Love is to die the death without awakening.

And he himself, the arch-magus, the Adept whose exalted energy makes him the monarch of rhythm in the murmuring universe of sounds, now holds in his right hand the key of power and of happiness. By the irresistible force, rightly directed, of the harmonics of sound—that is to say, of the electronic rhythm which, as modern science puts it, ensures with a perpetual movement the cohesion of molecules in all bodies, in animal, vegetable, and mineral life—he can flatten the menace of Jericho's impregnable walls, or raise serenely, like Amphion with the sound of his lyre, the walls of Thebes whose stones came and placed themselves in rhythm and in meter, one on top of the other.

By the science of the rhythm of the universe, he has become the equal of the Demiurge on the first day of creation.[82]

These passages give us a clue—nothing more—to the reality behind our subject. The vowels are the way in which the human being creates and perceives the phenomenon of harmonics. Subjectively speaking, harmonics are the foundations of number made audible. Objectively, they are the imposition of these numbers on the physical world. In making vowels, we are speaking or singing numbers. The physical world is nothing but number, and its laws are to a great extent harmonic ones. The "adept" of Mardrus's text is one who understands these laws, and can replicate them with the voice.

For this reason, I suspect that the original song of the vowels did not take the form of a scale, nor of seven vowels extracted from speech. I think its basis was not verbal or musical, but harmonic; that the vowels were used as a means of bringing to resonance the harmonics—perhaps the first seven, but more likely a wider range—and that these were focussed either internally, for the benefit of the singer, or externally, for healing and technical work. To the uninitiated listener, the harmonics would simply sound like vowels, and the pitches would be associated by the ear with the notes of a known scale. Hence the reports of classical authors, based on descriptions of the ritual song by those who had heard but not understood it, or as explained by the priests to the public, or, finally, as practiced by priests who had themselves lost its true meaning and effect.

Practical Exercises

Each of these exercises uses the vowels in a different way. No claims are made for them, least of all that any occult results will follow. But each has been found appropriate by some group, whether for mental or physical health, for consciousness expansion, or as a form of religious devotion. It is quite possible to choose and combine elements from all of them, to suit one's own inclinations. Although here, as in every kind of practical work, there are those who will insist that their method is the only valid one, the field of vowel-practice is in its second infancy, and there is plenty of room for experimentation.

1. Adapted from Dr. Hanish, *Cours d'Harmonie: l'Harmonie par le Chant* (Paris, Aryana, 1967).
Before World War I, Dr. Hanish was the founder of a movement called Mazdaznan, claiming a Zoroastrian tradition and emphasizing the power of the breath.

Breathe in by small amounts, as if you were sobbing.
Empty your lungs.
Breathe in again, sobbing as before.
Opening your mouth as wide as possible, sound the vowel
    calm [sound the vowel only: the word is given purely for
    guidance in pronunciation] and make it vibrate
    throughout your body, setting every part of it in vibration.

Repeat the exercise with the following vowels, in order:
    [calm] men hay eat (French) pur hood (French) voeu oh

77

Make the mouth positions for all the vowels firm, even exaggerated.

Perform the sequence once with an open mouth.
Perform them a second time, clenching the incisors.
Perform them a third time, clenching the molars.
Perform them a fourth time with the lips closed.

As you sound them, feel to your very fingertips the sentiments of each vowel:

calm expresses admiration, affirmation
men expresses refusal, disdain, defensiveness
hay is the vowel of astonishment, also equality and prac-
    ticality
eat is a state of lively joy and happiness
pur develops aesthetic awareness
hood is the vowel of interior research and metaphysics
voeu is research of the scientific order
oh awakens the religious sentiment and unites us to our
    Creator

Each vowel works on a different part of the spinal cord and a certain nerve-center. This work awakens all one's faculties and bears fruit in every department of life.

2. Adapted from William David, *The Harmonics of Sound, Color and Vibration: a System for Self-Awareness and Soul Evolution* (Marina del Rey, De Vorss, 1980).
The author was the founder, in 1970, of The Esoteric Philosophy Center, a school for new age education, in Houston, Texas.
For these exercises, stand erect with the feet shoulder-distance apart.

Sounding strongly the vowel *feet* (red), contemplate the qualities of freedom, will, power, strength, honor, determination, vitality, initiative, and action.
Gesture: hanging the arms down, bend the elbows to make

forearms parallel to floor; hands open. Pump forearms vigorously back and forth.

Sounding gently the vowel *oh* (blue), contemplate the qualities of love-wisdom, kindness, gentleness, humility, trust, understanding, self-forgiveness, compassion, patience, cooperation, and acceptance.

Gesture: make a circle with arms above head, entwining the fingers.

Sounding joyously the vowel *father* (yellow), contemplate joy, discipline, mental discrimination, evaluation, organization, justice, and harmony.

Gesture: stretch arms straight upward and forward, about 60° from horizontal, palms facing inward.

Sounding *fate* (green) expansively, contemplate same qualities as preceding two vowels, plus growth, expansion, healing, hope, enthusiasm, gratitude, creative communication.

Gesture: hold arms straight out to sides, forearms raised vertically, palms inward, to make a cup shape.

Sounding *let* (orange) with confidence, contemplate qualities of red and yellow plus courage, change, confidence, illumination, steadfastness, inventiveness, and intellect.

Gesture: extend arms forward about 30° from horizontal, palms inward.

Sounding softly *who* (purple-violet), contemplate red and blue qualities plus devotion, release, idealism, loyalty and responsibility.

Gesture: make a cup with the hands by facing palms outward, extending thumbs inwards and touching under the chin. Good for sense of self-acceptance and release from guilt.

Sounding *home* (indigo) in balance, giving O and M equal time, contemplate synthesis, unity, ritual, mastery, and ceremonial magic.

Gesture: legs about 60° apart, arms extended from shoulders to sides, about 60°, to make body a five-pointed star.

3. Adapted from Hélène Foglio, *Approches de l'Univers Sonore. Mantras—Sons—Phonèmes* (Paris, Le Courrier du Livre, 1985).

These exercises are included especially for the series of nasal resonances, a dimension neglected by most practitioners. The "internal massage" achieved through the powerful sounding of nasalized vowels is an exhilarating experience.

Sitting erect, breathe slowly and deeply, filling the lungs from the bottom upwards.

Hold the breath for six seconds, feel the accumulated prana, then breathe out sounding the vowels in order and feeling the appropriate emotional climate. Each one resonates in a different part of the body:

> A induces states of calm, peace, serenity. It resonates at the top of the thorax and the esophagus.
>
> E develops self-confidence. It resonates in the neck, vocal cords, sockets of the incisors, thyroid glands.
>
> I, the vowel of laughter, humor, and gaiety, stablizes humor. It is an ascending vowel, resonating in the bridge of the nose and the crown of the head.
>
> O turns inward and gives a sensation of seriousness, completion and perfection. It vibrates in the lower thorax and upper abdomen.
>
> OU has the same climate of gravity, but with a certain sweetness. It vibrates in the lower abdomen.

Nasal Resonance

Sitting with crossed legs, sound each vowel in turn, progressively nasalizing it by opening the soft palate. Thus transform A into a sort of ANG, and the other vowels accordingly.

Be careful to keep the shoulders relaxed as you do this, as they may otherwise tense up.

Repeat the exercise, beginning nasally and returning the vowels to their normal state.

Repeat the exercise, beginning normally, opening the nasal resonance, then returning in a single breath.

Since the interior of the nose replicates in miniature all the parts of the body [compare the therapies based on the foot, the hand, the ear, or the iris as corresponding to the entire body], this internal massage through sound has a most beneficial effect.

4. Adapted from Dr. J. L. Schmidt, as summarized in Peter Michael Hamel, trans. Peter Lemesurier, *Through Music to the Self* (Tisbury, Compton Press, 1978).

Hamel's book, like the others cited in this chapter, contains many more suggestions for practice in making and listening to sound.

For individual or group practice, in a state of relaxation.

Breathe in with a sigh and hold the breath; while holding it, open the mouth wide to the position of the vowel to be sung. To start with: A. Mouth big, wide open, round. The opening should be able to be felt right down past the jaw socket and into the back of the throat.

With the accumulated breath, the vowel A is now uttered, sounding in the prepared spaces and cavities until all the breath is used up. Wait a little while; breathe in deeply and repeat the vowel seven times in succession. Repeat the whole procedure with E, I, Ue, Oe (roughly 'Er'), O, U (OO) and M.

Also use this exercise making a crescendo on each vowel, and perhaps ending it with a final hum. Finally, take a very deep breath, briefly hold it, concentrate on the heart, and sing OM during the slow, gentle outbreath.

5. Adapted from Karlheinz Stockhausen, *Stimmung* (Vienna, Universal Edition, 1969).

Like many of Stockhausen's compositions, this one makes demands on the executant that are on the brink of impossibility, yet which introduce one, in the very act of attempting the impossible, to new realms of acoustical and temporal consciousness.

The instructions for the performers of this work include a table of the harmonics that can be brought to prominence by the different vowels. The symbols are those of the International Phonetic Association, London. The numbers above the symbols show the (approximate) harmonic sounded by a low female voice, e.g., at pitch 285 Hz (d' above Middle C); the numbers below, those of a low male voice, e.g., at 114 Hz (B♭ below Tenor C). The word-equivalents are the author's. Stockhausen says that it is advisable to practice by starting with the lowest vowel, and slowly working up one side or another of the table. With appropriate mouth, lip, and tongue position, every overtone from the 4th (or 2nd) to the 24th (or 12th) can be intoned separately.

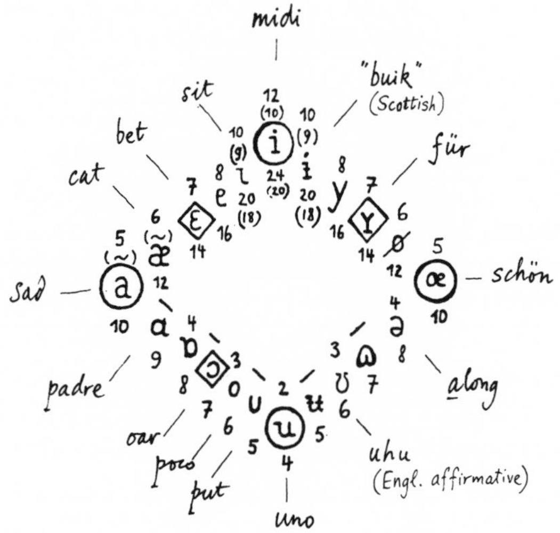

Illustration 1: Vowel scheme from *Stimmung*

6. From *The Light of the Intellect* by Abraham Abulafia, the Kabbalist. In Aryeh Kaplan, *Meditation and Kabbalah*. © Aryeh Kaplan, 1982. (York Beach, ME, Samuel Weiser, 1982), pp. 88–92. Used by permission.

This is not an exercise but a prayer, with mystical experience as its goal. It is included as an illustration of how close the Kabbalists came to speaking the forbidden name of Yahweh. In sounding every possible permutation of letters and vowel-points, the worshipper is, as it were, playing with fire: for if every possibility is tried, will he not eventually hit upon the true pronunciation, just as the monkeys with their typewriters will eventually write *Hamlet*? The instruction to prostrate oneself before any image that appears during practice also shows how far this is from exoteric Judaism and its commandments.

This is the mystery of how to pronounce the Glorious Name.

Make yourself right. Meditate in a special place, where your voice cannot be heard by others. Cleanse your heart and soul of all other thoughts in the world. Imagine that at this time, your soul is separating itself from your body, and that you are leaving the physical world behind, so that you enter the Future World, which is the source of all life distributed to the living.

[The Future World] is the intellect, which is the source of all Wisdom, Understanding and Knowledge, emanating from the King of Kings, the Blessed Holy One. All creatures fear Him with a great awe. This is the fear of one who actually perceives, and it is double the fear of one who merely has experienced love or awe.

Your mind must then come to join His Mind, which gives you the power to think. Your mind must divest itself of all other thoughts other than His Thought. This becomes like a partner, joining you to Him through His glorious, awesome Name.

You must therefore know precisely how to pronounce the Name. Its form [is given in the tables].

This is the technique. When you begin to pronounce the Alef with any vowel, it is expressing the mystery of Unity. You must therefore draw it out in one breath and no more. Do not interrupt this breath in any manner whatsoever until you have completed the pronunciation of the Alef.

Draw out this breath as long as you extend a single breath. At the same time, chant the Alef, or whatever other letter you are pronouncing, while depicting the form of the vowel point.

The first vowel is the *Cholem* (o, ̇), above the letter.

When you begin to pronounce it, direct your face toward the east, not looking up or down. You should be sitting, wearing clean, pure white robes over all your clothing, or else, wearing your prayer shawl over your head and crowned with your Tefillin. You must face the east, since it is from that direction that light emanates to the world.

With each of the twenty-five letter pairs, you must move your head properly.

When you pronounce the *Cholem* (o), begin facing directly east. Purify your thoughts, and as you exhale, raise your head, little by little, until when you finish, your head is facing upward. After you finish, prostrate yourself on the ground.

Do not interrupt between the breath associated with the Alef and the breath associated with the other letter in the pair. You may, however, take a single breath, and it may be long or short.

Between each pair of letters, you may take two breaths without making a sound, but not more than two. If you wish to take less than two breaths, you may do so.

After you finish each row, you may take five breaths, but no more. If you wish to take less, you may do so.

If you change anything or make any mistake in the order in any row, go back to the beginning of the row. Continue until you pronounce it correctly.

Just as you face upward when pronouncing the *Cholem*, face downward when you pronounce the *Chirek* (i, .). In this manner, you draw down the supernal power and bind it to yourself.

When you pronounce the *Shurek* (u, ̣ or ו), do not move your head upward or downward. Instead, move it straight forward (neither lowering or raising it).

When you pronounce the *Tzeré* (i, ̤), move your head from left to right.

When you pronounce the *Kametz* (a, ̣), move it from right to

Pronunciation with the Yod (י)

AoYo	AoYa	AoYe	AoYi	AoYu	אִי	אֵי	אֵיַ	אֶי	אֹי
AaYo	AaYa	AaYe	AaYi	AaYu	אַי	אַי	אַי	אַי	אָי
AeYo	AeYa	AeYe	AeYi	AeYu	אֶי	אֶי	אֶי	אֶי	אֶי
AiYo	AiYa	AiYe	AiYi	AiYu	אִי	אִי	אִי	אִי	אִי
AuYo	AuHa	AuYe	AuYi	AuYu	אֻי	אֻי	אֻי	אֻי	אֻי

YoAo	YoAa	YoAe	YoAi	YoAu	יֹא	יֹא	יֹא	יֹא	יֹא
YaAo	YaAa	YaAe	YaAi	YaAu	יָא	יָא	יָא	יָא	יָא
YeAo	YeAa	YeAe	YeAi	YeAu	יֶא	יֶא	יֶא	יֶא	יֶא
YiAo	YiAa	YiAe	YiAi	YiAu	יִא	יִא	יִא	יִא	יִא
YuAo	YuAa	YuAe	YuAi	YuAu	יֻא	יֻא	יֻא	יֻא	יֻא

Pronunciation with the Heh (ה)

AoHo	AoHa	AoHe	AoHi	AoHu	אֹה	אֹה	אֹה	אֹה	אֹה
AaHo	AaHa	AaHe	AaHi	AaHu	אָה	אָה	אָה	אָה	אָה
AeHo	AeHa	AeHe	AeHi	AeHu	אֶה	אֶה	אֶה	אֶה	אֶה
AiHo	AiHa	AiHe	AiHi	AiHu	אִה	אִה	אִה	אִה	אִה
AuHo	AuHa	AuHe	AuHi	AuHu	אֻה	אֻה	אֻה	אֻה	אֻה

HoAo	HoAa	HoAe	HoAi	HoAu	הֹא	הֹא	הֹא	הֹא	הֹא
HaAo	HaAa	HaAe	HaAi	HaAu	הָא	הָא	הָא	הָא	הָא
HeAo	HeAa	HeAe	HeAi	HeAu	הֶא	הֶא	הֶא	הֶא	הֶא
HiAo	HiAa	HiAe	HiAi	HiAu	הִא	הִא	הִא	הִא	הִא
HuAo	HuAa	HuAe	HuAi	HuAu	הֻא	הֻא	הֻא	הֻא	הֻא

Pronunciation with the Vav (ו)

AoVo	AoVa	AoVe	AoVi	AoVu	אֹו	אֹו	אֹו	אֹו	אֹו
AaVo	AaVa	AaVe	AaVi	AaVu	אָו	אָו	אָו	אָו	אָו
AeVo	AeVa	AeVe	AeVi	AeVu	אֶו	אֶו	אֶו	אֶו	אֶו
AiVo	AiVa	AiVe	AiVi	AiVu	אִו	אִו	אִו	אִו	אִו
AuVo	AuVa	AuVe	AuVi	AuVu	אֻו	אֻו	אֻו	אֻו	אֻו

VoAo	VoAa	VoAe	VoAi	VoAu	וֹא	וֹא	וֹא	וֹא	וֹא
VaAo	VaAa	VaAe	VaAi	VaAu	וָא	וָא	וָא	וָא	וָא
VeAo	VeAa	VeAe	VeAi	VeAu	וֶא	וֶא	וֶא	וֶא	וֶא
ViAo	ViAa	ViAe	ViAi	ViAu	וִא	וִא	וִא	וִא	וִא
VuAo	VuAa	VuAe	VuAi	VuAu	וֻא	וֻא	וֻא	וֻא	וֻא

Illustration 2: The tablets of the four letters
(The final Heh is identical to the earlier Heh sequence.)

left.

In any case, if you see any image before you, prostrate yourself before it immediately.

If you hear a voice, loud or soft, and wish to understand what it is saying, immediately respond and say, "Speak my Lord, for Your servant is listening" (I Samuel 3:9). Do not speak at all, but incline your ear to hear what is being said to you.

If you feel great terror and cannot bear it, prostrate yourself immediately, even in the middle of pronouncing a letter.

If you do not see or hear anything, do not use this technique again all that week.

It is good to pronounce this once each week, in a form that "runs and returns." For regarding this, a covenant has been made.

What can I add? What I have written is clear, and if you are wise, you will understand the entire technique.

If you feel that your mind is unstable, that your knowledge of Kabbalah is insufficient, or that your thoughts are bound to the vanities of the time, do not dare to pronounce the Name, lest you sin all the more.

Between the tablet of the Yod and that of the Heh, you can take twenty-five breaths, but no more. But you must not make any interruption at this time, not with speech and not with thought.

The same is true between the Heh and the Vav, and between the Vav and the final Heh. But if you wish to take less than twenty-five breaths, you may do so.

7. This is not so much an exercise as a description of the kind of singing practiced in many groups and workshops. It is given here to encourage others to explore this spontaneous improvisation, which may indeed be the "Song of the Vowels" best suited to the present time.

Lights are dimmed, eyes are closed. There may be only six people, standing in a circle, their feet gently planted, hands hanging loosely by their sides. Or there may be two hundred people sitting in a hall, comfortable but poised, like Egyptian statues. They breathe deeply, listening only to the sound of their own breath.

After a while, the breathing silence is broken by a moan, no louder than the wind makes. Another answers it, eager for expression. These are the first quickenings of tones seeking to be born. No one knows who started them, and nobody cares. We are leaving the world of personalities behind, as we begin our journey into the tone-world.

How readily the gruff sounds assemble, align, and merge into the first communal tones! This is nobody's doing, simply the way of Nature, obedient to the laws of harmony, and of ears designed to share her delight in simple numbers.

But no self-respecting Demiurge would create a universe out of concord alone. To set a world rolling, it takes the polarity of discord, the sour apple of Eve or the golden apple of Eris. Then the human race is thrown out of Eden to earn its own living, or sets off to fight its Trojan wars. It is the same in even the simplest music. One can be sure that someone in the circle will provide the daemonic element, singing off-key or performing a long slow glissando, and turn the harmonious hums to chaos. Apollo must periodically give way to Dionysus.

The faint-hearted are disquieted by this nigredo of collective cries and groans. Haven't they heard enough cacophony outside this enchanted company? But it needs the alembic of noise to prepare a new elixir of concord, one perhaps spiced with a bolder flavor, vibrant with a more volatile energy.

One has the feeling that something is being built with this mobile architecture of tone, the counterpart of the "frozen music" of the cathedral builders. Each person works on a different part of the structure. The possessor of a deep bass voice can rest at the foundation, enjoying the play of the others above him. In a small choir, he can choose to slide around a little and unseat the whole construction; he can descend a fifth and give it a profounder resonance; or he can attempt the super-low tones of organs and Tibetan chanters.

The pleasure is different in the middle ranges of tenor and alto, where the voice can be focused and sent slicing through the very center of the sound. Here it may meet with a companion, or a rival, and the two of them can weave an ephemeral duet. But the greatest glory is reserved for the higher voices that sail joyfully on this unstable sea, soaring in the tonal aether like birds or like angels.

As the song goes on, some people hear strange things, especially in large groups: Gregorian chanting, hidden orchestras, inhuman or superhuman voices. Once they realize that no one is listening to them, everyone becomes more adventurous. Those who can produce voice harmonics add them as an embellishment to the ensemble; those who couldn't may now try. Women find new depths to their voices, men rise to the falsetto range. There are no wrong notes, since every element, even the apparently ugly, can be absorbed and woven into the whole.

Fresh colors beam forth as the commonplace Ah's and Oh's give place to the sharper vowels and nasal tones: the grinning Eee, the French U with its bouquet of high harmonics, the sawtooth Zzz, the electrifying Ng that clears the sinuses and shakes the floor of the brain.

Someone tries to start up a rhythm. Will the others join the dance? Once inhibitions are laid aside, the most bizarre things may happen: the whole choir may turn itself for a while into a surreal band. As that energy gives out, and almost shamefacedly the beat withers away, the music nearly dies; yet one or two singers are still reluctant to return from the world of the ear to that of the eye. The ups and downs of collective energy are unaccountable, but often the most sublime moments occur in a swelling final chorus, as each takes a last chance to enjoy a mode of existence that they know they must soon leave.

After that comes a silence profound and rich, like the silence after love. How better could you make love to six people, or to six hundred, than by singing with them?

Surely this is the primordial song of the human race and the musical birthright of us all. Such music may have echoed in the caves of Lascaux, or in the temples of Atlantis; it can manifest wherever there are voices and ears. The laws of harmony which it intuitively obeys are as immutable as the laws of mathematics. It transcends all the artificial barriers that clutter the musical field. It is a-historical, neither 'classical' nor 'popular'. It requires no one to be paid or praised for it; composer, performer, and listener are one. It unites professionals with amateurs, the musically literate with the ignorant. Most gratifying of all, people who believed that they could not sing have discovered their own voices through it, and found that they are beautiful.

Notes

1. See Paget, *Human Speech*, p. 90. It is an unfortunate fact that every Britisher carries a conscious or unconscious vowel-meter with which to measure the social rank of any speaker, the vowels of Paget's "Southern English" accent being the cynosure of respectablility. This is perhaps why the English are more sensitive to the subject of vowels than citizens of less class-ridden nations.

2. Dayton Miller's lectures were given in 1914 and subsequently reprinted in *The Science of Musical Sounds*. This controversy is explained on pp. 217ff.

3. Paget, p. 40.

4. Ibid., p. 97.

5. Miller, p. 226.

6. See the comparative chart added by Alexander Ellis to his translation of Helmholtz, *On the Sensations of Tone as a Physiological Basis for the Theory of Music*, p. 109n.

7. See Barthélemy's "Remarques sur les médailles d'Antonin, frappées en Egypte."

8. See Dornseiff, *Das Alphabet in Mystik und Magie*, p. 41. This work contains the richest documentation of the subject.

9. See Bidez, *Vie de Porphyre*, appendix, p. 72. I am grateful to Stephen Ronan for this clarification, as for much else concerning the vowels in Antiquity.

10. Irenaeus, *Against Heresies*, I, xiv, in *The Writings of Irenaeus*, vol. I, pp. 56ff.

11. Eusebius, *Praeparatio Evangelica* V, xiv, 1.

12. Ibid., XI. vi, 36.

13. Ibid., sect. 37.

14. Dornseiff, p. 44.

15. On the Sabaeans, see Nick Kollerstrom, "The Star Temples of Harran."

16. Demetrius *On Style*, II, 71; Loeb edition, p. 347. The translator, W. Rhys Roberts, believes the author to be Demetrius of Tarsus, late first century C.E., rather than Demetrius of Phalerum, fourth century B.C.E., to whom the work is usually attributed. The interest in Egyptian religion is certainly characteristic of the age of Plutarch.

17. On the symbolic meaning of phonemes in Hebrew, see Fabre d'Olivet, *La Langue Hébraïque réstituée*. On those of Arabic and Sanskrit, see Jean Canteinas, *Phonèmes et Archétypes*.

18. See especially Garth Fowden, *The Egyptian Hermes*. Fowden's scholarly argument goes some way toward reinstating the credibility of G. R. S. Mead, who in *Thrice Greatest Hermes* argued against accepted opinion for the Egyptian origin of Hermetic thought.

19. Communication of Mr. Ronan to the author, October 1989. For further ramifications of the subject, see his "Theodorus of Asine and the Kabbalah" and his edition of Porphyry's *On the Symbolism of the Gods*.

20. Nicomachus of Gerasa, *Harmonicum enchiridion* in von Jan's *Musici Scriptores Graeci*, p. 276, 8ff. Translation from Stephen Gersh, *From Iamblichus to Eriugena*, p. 295.

21. Nicomachus of Gerasa, *Theologumena arithmeticae* 71.

22. Translated by G. R. S. Mead, *Fragments of a Faith Forgotten*, p. 363; Irenaeus, ed. cit., vol. I, p. 56f.

23. Irenaeus, ed. cit., pp. 60f.

24. Mead, op. cit., pp. 368-73; Irenaeus, ed. cit., pp. 62f.

25. In George Boas's translation of *The Hieroglyphics of Horapollo*, p. 91, hieroglyphic II, 29 reads: "Seven letters surrounded by two fingers mean a muse, the infinite, or fate."

26. Barthélemy, op. cit., p. 188.

27. Kopp, *Palaeographia critica*, pt. iii, sects. 250-291.

28. From Escudier, *Dictionnaire de Musique*, s.v. "Phoeniciens, Musique des," there attributed to Fabre d'Olivet. See my transla-

tion of his *La musique expliquée comme science et comme art*, pp. 162-3.

29. See Fabre d'Olivet's *Histoire philosophique du genre humain*, especially vol. I, ch. 5.

30. In *Mathematische Philosophie*. I take this summary of J. J. Wagner's vowel theory from a lecture by Prof. Antoine Faivre at the Ecole Pratique des Hautes Etudes, Paris, 1986.

31. Further on the symbolism of the three letters or key-vowels A-I-U, see Jean Canteinas, *Phonèmes et Archétypes* and *La Voie des Lettres*; also the extremely rare work of Ange Pechméja, *L'Oeuf de Kneph—Histoire secrète du Zéro*. I am grateful to David Fideler and to Jean-Pierre Brach for these references.

32. Jean Thamar, "Notion de la musique traditionnelle," in *Etudes Traditionelles*, no. 270 (1948), p. 252n.

33. See Godwin, *Harmonies of Heaven and Earth*, pp. 181f.

34. Robert Greer Cohn, *The Poetry of Rimbaud*, p. 130. Cohn's is the most balanced commentary on this poem, which has given rise to some extremes of doctrinal interpretation.

35. The Dragon's Tail and Head are the astrological terms for the South and North nodes of the Moon's orbit. By including them both, the planet Saturn is left out.

36. Hargrave Jennings, *The Rosicrucians, their Rites and Mysteries*, p. 174.

37. See "Les sons et la lumière astrale," in P. Sédir, *Les Incantations*, pp. 179-95, with illustrations.

38. See Maurice Tuchman, ed., *The Spiritual in Art: Abstract Painting 1890-1985*.

39. Cyril Scott, *The Philosophy of Modernism*, pp. 115-6 (Appendix I on "The Occult Relationship between Sound and Colour").

40. Isaac Newton added "indigo" to the three primary and three secondary colors known to painters, apparently out of a desire to make the divisions of the spectrum correspond with the seven notes of the scale. See his *Opticks*, Bk. I, pt. II, Prop. III, prob. I. On the consequences of this for music and color theory, see Chapter I of my forthcoming *L'Esotérisme musical en France, 1750-1950*.

41. Vincent's *Réponse à M. Fétis . . .*, p. 57.

42. C. Parthey, "Zwei griechische Zauberpapyri des Berliner Museums."

43. C. -E. Ruelle, "Le chant des sept voyelles grecques d'après Démétrius et les papyrus de Leyde."

44. C. -E. Ruelle, "Le Chant gnostico-magique des sept voyelles grecques, esquisse historique," and Elie Poirée, "Le Chant gnostico-magique des sept voyelles grecques, analyse musicale."

45. Egon Wellesz, "Music in the Treatises of Greek Gnostics and Alchemists." The quotation is from p. 151.

46. Hans Dieter Betz, ed., *The Greek Magical Papyri in Translation, including the Demotic Spells.*

47. *The Nag Hammadi Library in English*, p. 296. Another version of the incantation is in Kurt Rudolph, *Gnosis*, p. 224.

48. A. B. Klein, *Colour-Music: the Art of Light*, p. 243; see also Raymond Rudorff, *The Belle Epoque—Paris in the Nineties*, pp. 143-4.

49. Armande de Polignac, "Musique de scène"; quotation from p. 71.

50. Notably on 8 May 1910, at a concert Bailly organized at the Theosophical Society of France in commemoration of the death of Mme. Blavatsky.

51. See pp. 26 and 24 of *Le Chant des Voyelles.*

52. Bailly writes (ibid., p. 31): "*a, i, u*" but the last letter is surely a misprint for *ou*. Beside the evidence of fact, the end of the song amply supports this emendation.

53. Ibid., p. 5.

54. H. P. Blavatsky, *The Secret Doctrine*, Adyar ed., vol. I, pp. 136ff.

55. See Alexandre Scriabine, *Notes et Réflexions: Carnets inédits*, p. 121 et passim.

56. Neptune's orbit formed the known boundary of the solar system until the discovery of Pluto in 1930.

57. But see the sixth exercise in our Chapter 10, where a medieval Kabbalist gives instructions that come perilously close to sounding the Name.

58. Fabre d'Olivet, *La Langue Hébraïque Restituée*, vol. I, p. 19.

59. *Saturnalia* I, 18, quoting Apollinus Clarinus.

60. P. E. Jablonski, *Pantheon Aegyptiorum*, pp. 250-4.

61. G. Higgins, *The Celtic Druids*, pp. 196f.

62. See Godfrey Higgins, *Anacalypsis*, vol. I, pp. 323-331 for all the following citations.

63. But see *Anacalypsis*, vol. II, p. 151 on EVOHE as a lunar word.

64. G. R. S. Mead, *Fragments of a Faith Forgotten*, p. 534.

65. From Jean Robin, *Les Sociétés secrètes au rendez-vous de l'Apocalypse*, p. 44.

66. See *The Nag Hammadi Library in English*, pp. 195-205.

67. For an extract from the work of von Thimus, see my *Harmony of the Spheres: A Sourcebook*.

68. Paul Vulliaud, "Première Mystagogique."

69. Idid., p. 300. I leave the first phrase untranslated because English has only one word where French has three.

70. A. Lethierry-Barrois, *Hébreu Primitif*, p. 1.

71. *Le Papisme et la Civilisation*, vol. II, pp. 28-9.

72. Ibid., pp. 34-5.

73. Ibid., p. 40.

74. *The Secret Doctrine*, Adyar ed., vol. I, p. 136.

75. Ibid., vol. II, p. 168.

76. See especially *Fragments of a Faith Forgotten*, consulting Index s. v. "Voices."

77. Blavatsky, vol. II, p. 127.

78. See Paul Brunton, *A Search in Secret Egypt*, pp. 281-3.

79. From Fidèle Amy-Sage, "Le secret de la sépulture d'un Pharaon."

80. On the seven laughs of the Creator, see two versions of the "Eighth Book of Moses," in Betz, ed., *The Greek Magical Papyri in Translation*, pp. 176ff, 185ff.

81. However, it can still happen even in our century. For an eyewitness account by the Swedish aircraft designer Henry Kjellson, who saw large stones levitated several hundred feet by means of music by a group of Tibetan monks, see Playfair and Hill, *The Cycles of Heaven*, pp. 137-140.

82. From Mardrus, *La Toute-Puissance de l'Adepte*, pp. 79ff.

Le Chant des Voyelles
by Edmond Bailly

Bailly writes in preface to this score: ". . . the accompaniment by Harps and Double Flutes, the latter scarcely found outside the cases of large museums, can be replaced by a harmonium (also flute, English horn); the combination of piano and harmonium is more satisfactory still. In the most frequent case, when only a piano is available, it is essential to distinguish the two different sonorities of the accompaniment." (*Le Chant des Voyelles*, p. 32)

Bailly did not, of course, imagine that these seven French vowels are more than an approximation to those of the ancient Greeks or Egyptians. For speakers of other languages, it would be best to imitate his principle of fixing the "ideal triad" of A, I, and O, adding between them the most distinguishable vowels of one's own language.

If one wishes to conform with the reported Egyptian practice of alternating song with prayer, Bailly suggests the repetition of the piece minus the first four and last two measures, the latter being added only at the close of the ceremony. For a prayer, he adds, one might use the invocation made by Julius Firmicus Maternus on behalf of the Emperor Constantine (early 4th century C.E.):

O Sun, soul of the world, dwelling in the midst of the heavens, who by the wise dispensation of your light rules the ever-sparkling fires of the wandering stars; O Star of Night, earth's neighbor, who sustains the seeds enclosed in her bosom as they receive the august imprint of the Sun, who modifies them at your will, and by your changing phases heralds and causes the waxing and waning of beings; O Saturn, who from the summit of the heavens slowly pours upon us the rays with which you are crowned; O Jupiter, reigning alike on the Tarpeian Rock and in the second sphere of the heavens, who enlivens the earth and the whole world by the kind and majestic serenity of your glance; O you who rule in the third celestial region, Mars, whose terrible aspect inspires such fear among mortals; and you, Mercury and Venus, faithful companions of the Sun; we pray to you in favor of . . . [add the name or object of the invocation].

Le Chant des Voyelles

The Song of the Vowels

Reconstructed by EDMOND BAILLY

Bibliography

Amy-Sage, Fidèle. "Le secret de la sépulture d'un Pharaon," *Le Voile d'Isis*, 1923, 317ff.

Bailly, Edmond. *Le Chant des Voyelles comme invocation aux dieux planétaires, suivi d'une restitution vocale avec accompagnement*. Paris, L'Art Indépendant, 1912. Reprinted Nice, Bélisane, 1976.

Barthélemy, Abbé Jean Jacques. "Remarques sur les médailles d'Antonin, frappées en Egypte," *Mémoires de l'Académie des Inscriptions et Belles-Lettres*, 41 (1775), 514ff. Also in his *Oeuvres diverses*. 2 vols., Paris, 1798.

[Bertet, Alphonse] Le Paysan de Saint Pierre. *Le Papisme et la Civilisation au Tribunal de l'Evangile Eternel*. Chambéry, Ménard & Cie., 1870.

Betz, Hans Dieter, ed. *The Greek Magical Papyri in Translation, including the Demotic Spells*. University of Chicago Press, 1986.

Bidez, J. *Vie de Porphyre*. Ghent, 1913.

Blavatsky, H. P. *The Secret Doctrine*. 6 vols. Adyar, Theosophical Publishing House, 1971.

Brunton, Paul. *A Search in Secret Egypt*. New York, Dutton, 1936.

Canteinas, Jean. *La Voie des Lettres*. Paris, Albin Michel, 1982.

——. *Phonèmes et Archétypes*. Paris, Maisonneuve et Larose, 1972.

Cohn, Robert Greer. *The Poetry of Rimbaud*. Princeton University Press, 1970.

David, William. *The Harmonics of Sound, Color and Vibration: a System for Self-Awareness and Soul Evolution*. Marina del Rey, De Vorss, 1980.

Demetrius. *On Style*, trans. W. Rhys Roberts. London, Heinemann, 1927.

Dornseiff, Franz. *Das Alphabet in Mystik und Magie.* 2nd ed. Leipzig, Teubner, 1925.

Escudier, J. and M. *Dictionnaire de Musique.* Paris, 1844.

Eusebius. *Praeparatio Evangelica.*

Fabre D'Olivet. *Histoire philosophique du genre humain.* 2 vols. Paris, 1822. Trans. N. L. Redfield as *Hermeneutic Interpretation of the Origin of the Social State of Man.* New York, G. P. Putnam's Sons, 1915.

——. *La Langue Hébraïque réstituée.* 2 vols. Paris, 1815–16. Trans. Nayán Louise Redfield as *The Hebrew Tongue Restored.* New York, G. P. Putnam's Sons, 1918.

——. *La musique expliquée comme science et comme art.* Trans. Joscelyn Godwin as *Music explained as science and art.* Rochester, VT, Inner Traditions International, 1987.

Foglio, Hélène. *Approches de l'Univers Sonore. Mantras—Sons— Phonèmes.* Paris, Le Courrier du Livre, 1985.

Fowden, Garth. *The Egyptian Hermes.* Cambridge, University Press, 1986.

Gersh, Stephen. *From Iamblichus to Eriugena.* Leiden, Brill, 1978.

Godwin, Joscelyn. *L'Esotérisme musical en France, 1750–1950.* Paris, Albin Michel, forthcoming.

——. *Harmonies of Heaven and Earth.* London, Thames & Hudson, 1987.

——. *Harmony of the Spheres: A Sourcebook.* Rochester, VT, Inner Traditions International, 1990.

Hamel, Peter Michael. *Through Music to the Self.* Trans. Peter Lemesurier. Tisbury, Compton Press, 1978.

Hanish, Dr. *Cours d'Harmonie: l'Harmonie par le Chant.* Paris, Aryana, 1967.

Helmholtz, Hermann L. F., *On the Sensations of Tone as a Physiological Basis for the Theory of Music*, trans. Alexander J. Ellis. London, 1885. Reprinted New York, Dover, 1954.

Higgins, Godfrey. *Anacalypsis: An Attempt to Draw Aside the Veil of the Saitic Isis; or an Inquiry into the Origin of Languages,*

Nations and Religions. 2 vols. London, 1833, 1836. 2nd ed. New York, Macy-Masius, 1927.

———. *The Celtic Druids.* London, 1829. Reprinted Los Angeles, Philosophical Research Society, 1977.

Horapollo. *The Hieroglyphics of Horapollo,* trans. George Boas. New York, Bollingen Foundation, 1950.

Irenaeus. *The Writings of Irenaeus,* trans. Alexander Roberts and W. H. Rambaut. *The Ante-Nicene Christian Library.* Edinburgh, 1868.

Jablonski, P. E. *Pantheon Aegyptiorum.* Frankfurt A. M., 1750.

Jan, Carl von. *Musici Scriptores Graeci.* Leipzig, Teubner, 1895.

Jennings, Hargrave. *The Rosicrucians, their Rites and Mysteries.* London, J. C. Hotten, 1870.

Kaplan, Aryeh. *Meditation and Kabbalah.* York Beach, Maine, Weiser, 1982.

Klein, Adrian Bernard. *Colour-Music: the Art of Light.* 2nd ed. London, Crosby Lockwood, 1930.

Kollerstrom, Nick. "The Star Temples of Harran," *History and Astrology; Clio and Urania confer,* ed. Annabella Kitson. London, Unwin, 1989.

Kopp, Ulrich. *Palaeographia critica.* Mannheim, 1829.

Lethierry-Barrois, A. *Hébreu Primitif; formation des lettres ou chiffres, signes du zodiaque et racines hébraïques avec leurs dérivés dans les langues de l'Orient et de l'Europe.* Paris, A. Franck, 1867.

Mardrus, Joseph-Charles-Victor. *La Toute-Puissance de l'Adepte. Transcription des Hauts Textes Initiatiques de l'Egypte. Le Livre de la Vérité de Parole.* Paris, Bibliothèque Eudiaque, 1932.

Mead, G. R. S. *Fragments of a Faith Forgotten.* 2nd ed. London, Theosophical Publishing Society, 1906.

———. "Theosophical Symbology," *Theosophical Siftings,* 3 (1890).

———. *Thrice Greatest Hermes.* 3 vols. London, Theosophical Publishing Society, 1906.

Miller, Dayton Clarence. *The Science of Musical Sounds.* 2nd ed. New York, Macmillan, 1937.

[Nag Hammadi] *The Nag Hammadi Library in English,* general ed.

James M. Robinson. San Francisco, Harper & Row, 1977.

Paget, Sir Richard, Bt. *Human Speech*. New York, Harcourt, Brace & Co., 1930.

Parthey, Gustav Friedrich. "Zwei griechische Zauberpapyri des Berliner Museums," *Abhandlungen der Königlichen Akademie der Wissenschaften zu Berlin; Philologische-historische Klasse,* 1865, 109–80.

Pechmeja, Ange. *L'Oeuf de Kneph—Histoire secrète du Zéro.* Bucharest, 1864. The only extant copy appears to be in the Bibliothèque Nationale, Paris.

Playfair, Guy L. and Scott Hill. *The Cycles of Heaven*. New York, St. Martin's Press, 1978.

Poirée, Elie. "Le Chant gnostico-magique des sept voyelles grecques, analyse musicale," *Congrès international d'histoire de la Musique* (Paris, 1900), 28–38.

Polignac, Armande de. "Musique de scène," *La Rénovation,* December 1905, 69ff.

Porphyry. *On the Symbolism of the Gods,* ed. S. Ronan, forthcoming.

Robin, Jean. *Les Sociétés secrètes au rendez-vous de l'Apocalypse.* Paris, Guy Trédaniel, 1985.

Ronan, Stephen. "Theodorus of Asine and the Kabbalah," *Hermetic Journal* 42 (1988), 25–35.

Rudolph, Kurt. *Gnosis,* trans. Robert McLachan Wilson. Edinburgh, T. & T. Clark, 1983.

Rudorff, Raymond. *The Belle Epoque—Paris in the Nineties*. New York, Saturday Review Press, 1973.

Ruelle, Charles Emile. "Le chant des sept voyelles grecques d'après Démétrius et les papyrus de Leyde," *Revue des études grecques,* 1888, 38–44.

———. "Le Chant gnostico-magique des sept voyelles grecques, esquisse historique," *Congrès international d'histoire de la Musique* (Paris, 1900), 15–27.

Scott, Cyril. *The Philosophy of Modernism*. London, Waverley Book Co., nd.

Scriabine, Alexandre. *Notes et Réflexions: Carnets inédits,* ed. and trans. Marina Scriabine. Paris, Klincksieck, 1979.

Sédir, Paul. *Les Incantations.* Paris, Chamuel, 1897.

Stockhausen, Karlheinz. *Stimmung.* Vienna, Universal Edition, 1969.

Thamar, Jean. "Notion de la musique traditionnelle," *Etudes Traditionnelles,* Nos. 263–271 (1947–48).

Tuchman, Maurice, ed. *The Spiritual in Art: Abstract Painting 1890–1985.* Los Angeles County Museum of Art, 1986.

Vincent, Alexandre-Joseph-Hidulph. *Réponse à M.Fétis et réfutation de son mémoire sur cette question: Les Grecs et les Romains ont-ils connu l'harmonie simultanée des sons? et ont-ils fait usage dans leur musique?* Lille, Danel, 1859.

Vulliaud, Paul. "Première Mystagogique: Principes généraux et Applications. Cosmosophie Musicale," *Les Entretiens Idéalistes* 5/33 (25 June 1909), 281–7, 298–305.

Wagner, J. J. *Mathematische Philosophie.* Erlangen, 1811.

Wellesz, Egon. "Music in the Treatises of Greek Gnostics and Alchemists," *Ambix* 4/3+4 (1951), 145–58.

PHANES PRESS both publishes and distributes many fine books which relate to the philosophical, religious, and spiritual traditions of the Western world. To obtain a copy of our current catalogue, please write:

PHANES PRESS
PO BOX 6114
GRAND RAPIDS, MI 49516
USA

You can also find our entire catalogue
on the World Wide Web at:

http://www.phanes.com